MYANMAR AND ITS STRATEGIC DILEMMAS

MYANMAR AND ITS STRATEGIC DILEMMAS

Mohinder Pal Singh, Ph.D

PENTAGON PRESS

Myanmar and its Strategic Dilemmas
by Mohinder Pal Singh

First Published in 2018

ISBN 978-93-86618-56-6

Published by
PENTAGON PRESS
206, Peacock Lane, Shahpur Jat
New Delhi-110049
Phones: 011-64706243, 26491568
Telefax: 011-26490600
email: rajan@pentagonpress.in
website: www.pentagonpress.in

Printed at Aegean Offset Printers, Greater Noida, U.P.

CONTENTS

PREFACE

The almost three decade relationship between China and Myanmar is best characterised as a nuptial knot of convenience rather than of adoration. The inter-dependence to a great extent is asymmetric – Myanmar knows that it has much more to lose should the relationship with this giant neighbour snap. China has been its protector in the Security Council against human rights resolution and it's also a key economic partner and a source of large scale investment. China , which is landlocked from the south is looking for a smooth landbridge to the Indian Ocean and Myanmar provides one such viable option. While China sees some minor problems with the onset of democracy and the opening of Myanmar's markets to many other countries, it feels it can still continue to protect its economic and strategic interests in the country as other nations have not really made any big foray in Myanmar's economy.

India on the other hand in the last two decades played an important role in supporting the pro-democracy movement while engaging with the military rulers. India's support of Aung San Suu Kyi fructified in 2015 elections in which full restoration of Democracy took place and for the first time in 60 years a civilian government came to power. India has been engaging with Myanmar with full support to the new government.

On the other hand Myanmar , as a nation which is sandwiched between the two giant neighbours India and China which are strong regional powers wants to maintain its neutrality. Myanmar has always been cautious about the potential threat from rising China. Myanmar is now trying to diversify its external relations with India, Russia, Japan and ASEAN countries for the sake of attaining alternatives to mitigate its over-dependence on China. To a much larger extent it seems to be succeeding and world is witnessing a slow but steady emergence of a new Myanmar which is going to be a responsible democracy in the region.

Mohinder Pal Singh

ABBREVIATIONS

AFPFL	Anti Fascist People's Freedom League
BCIM	Bangladesh, China, India, Myanmar
BDA	Burma Defence Army
BIA	Burma Independence Army
BIMSTEC	Bay of Bengal Initiative for Multi-Sectoral Technical and Economic Cooperation
BNA	Burma National Army
BSPP	Burmese Socialist Program Party
CMC	Central Military Commission
CNPC	China National Petroleum Corporation
CPB	Communist Party of Burma
EU	European Union
IMET	The International Military Education and Training
KMMTTP	Kaladan Multi-Modal Transit Transport Project
KMT	Kuomintang
KNU	Karen National Union
LDC	Least developed countries
LEP	Look East Policy
LOC	Line of Credit
MNDAA	Myanmar National Democratic Alliance Army
MOGE	Myanmar Oil and Gas Enterprise

NLD	National League of Democracy
PLAN	Peoples Liberation Army Navy
SLOC	Sea lines of communication
SLORC	State Law and Order Restoration Council
TCF	Trillion Cubic Feet
UNSC	United Nations Security Council
YMBA	Yong Mens Buddhist Association

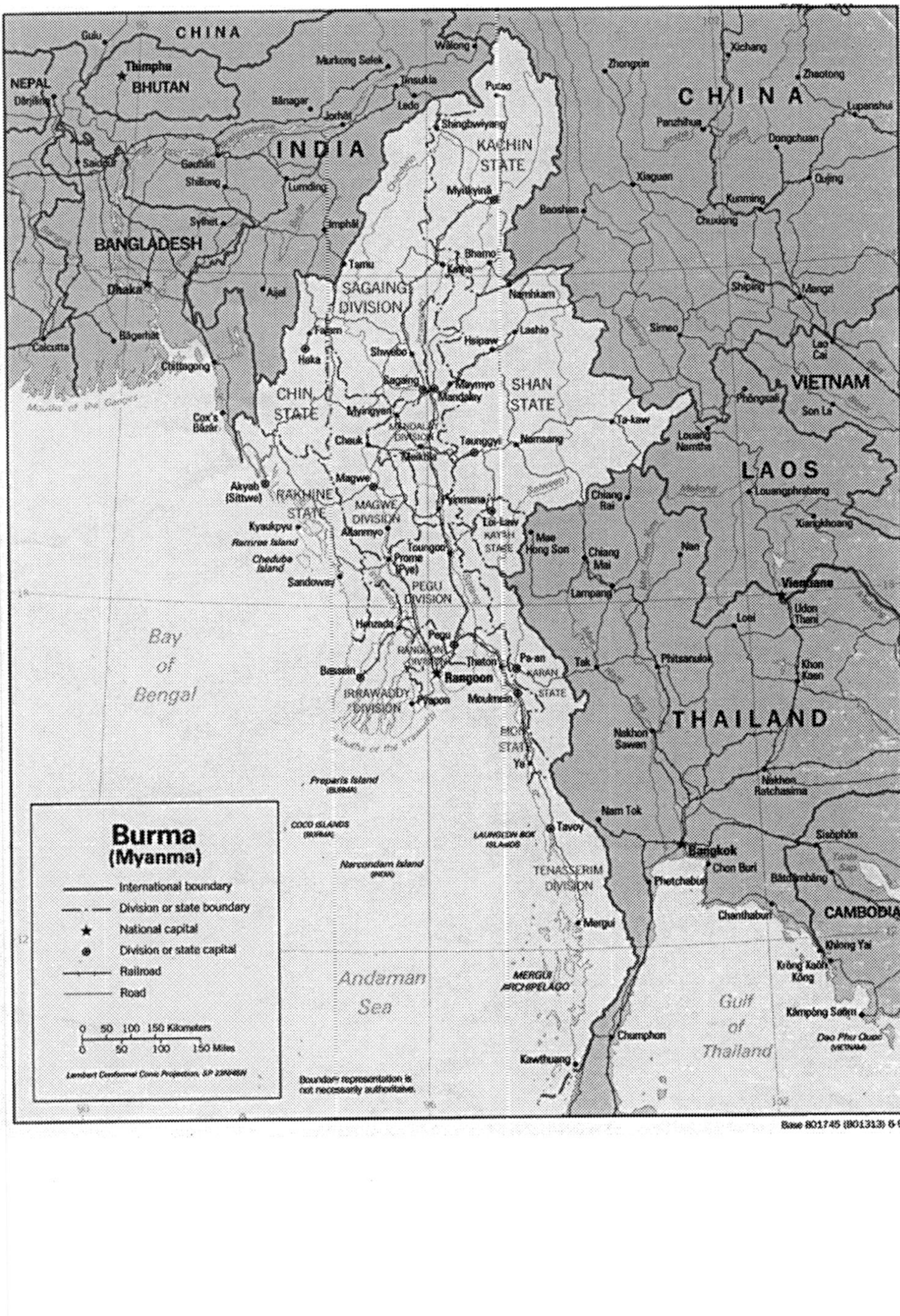

Base 801745 (801313) 6-91

1

INTRODUCTION

Relations between China-Myanmar and India-Myanmar have been in the forefront for the last two decades mainly due to the increased geo-political significance of Myanmar for the two Asian giants. However, the influence of China on the military government of Myanmar as well as the protection provided by China in thwarting any UN sanctions have recently become a hot topic in international relations. It was evident that China was the most important foreign actor in Myanmar after the 1990s when the Western countries (mainly the USA, EU and Japan) imposed strict sanctions against Myanmar in trade and economic ties.

In the mid-Nineties, India became vary of seeing China at its eastern doorstep and as part of its 'Look East Policy' increased its engagement with the military junta of Myanmar. This continued for next two decades when the military *junta* formed a new constitution which gave them tremendous powers and conducted an election based on it. The election was believed to have been rigged and was boycotted by the main opposition party, i.e., the National League of Democracy (NLD) led by Nobel Laureate Aung San Suu Kyi. As a result, the military-backed political party, the USDP came to power. Though its government was led by ex-general Thein Sein, he began sowing seeds of reform and the political environment began to change after 2011.

This action increased international engagement resulting in the partial lifting of sanctions by many countries, including the USA. However because of its massive investments, China still made a large influence on Naypyidaw in comparison with other countries, especially its western neighbour, India. Government-to-government cooperation between Myanmar and China became substantial as the latter repeatedly blocked UN Security Council resolutions against Myanmar on the issue of human rights. In addition, China increased its ties with Myanmar in many vital areas like military hardware, infrastructure and border trade. However, there are some thorns in the bilateral relations like environmental hazards being envisaged in the China-backed $3.2 billion Myitsone dam project with local residents opposing it. Succumbing to pressure from the local bodies in Myanmar, work on the dam was stopped by the Myanmar government in 2013. Also, the aspect of Chinese links with various ethnic groups in Myanmar was seriously affecting the relationship. Political developments after the visit of the US President in 2013 and other leading politicians and officials from the United States, EU and Japan and the aid promised by them to some extent undermined the Chinese position in Myanmar.

This book will try to analyze the Chinese role and influence in Myanmar as well as study its effect on the growing India-Myanmar ties, especially with the return of full democracy in 2016 with the new regime led by Aung San Suu Kyi.

It is often suggested that Sino–Myanmar security relations have tremendously improved in recent years and rumours of forward-looking Chinese maritime bases in Myanmar remain just rumours without any confirmation from either side. It is true that an improvement in security relations has been seen, but only in the context of a general improvement in bilateral relations between Myanmar and China. This closeness is not without its limitations and China has had a difficult task in dealing with the Myanmar government on many issues. Myanmar too has been balancing China with other players in the region rather majestically.

China's influence on the Thein Sein leadership in Myanmar was evident to the world, but after the 2015 election and a serious change in the political environment in the country, the situation as to which way equations will emerge needs to be closely watched. Nevertheless, there is no doubt that China which has already invested over USD16 billion in various projects will not let the situation go out of control. It already has a pipeline pumping oil and gas into its poorly developed state of Yunnan. It will surely try to increase its influence at all levels in spite of the changed political environment in Myanmar. Anticipating this change, China had invited the opposition leader, Aung San Suu Kyi, to China in June 2015.

An increasing number of international actors are closely watching as to how the improved relationship between China and Myanmar will impact security relationships in South and Southeast Asia. The influence and strategic importance which China has in Myanmar is often exaggerated; China's rise is seen in a far too "positive" light, while the negative aspects of increased contacts are less apparent and often forgotten. The reality is that many dimensions of bilateral relations are tense and the Myanmar government is deliberately trying to balance different external actors against one another in order to minimize external pressures and maximize concessions.

2

HISTORICAL AND POLITICAL BACKDROP

Myanmar, officially known as the Union of Myanmar, is the largest country by area in mainland Southeast Asia. On 4 January 1948, Burma achieved independence from Great Britain and became the "Union of Burma." Subsequently, changes in its name were done and on 4 January 1974, it became "Socialist Republic of the Union of Burma"; on 23 September 1988, the "Union of Burma" and, since 18 June 1989, it is known as the "Union of Myanmar." Some countries which did not recognise the erstwhile ruling military *junta* continue to refer to it as Burma or the Union of Burma. Myanmar has got five land neighbours. It is bordered by the People's Republic of China on the north, Laos on the east, Thailand on the southeast, Bangladesh on the west and India on the northwest. One-third of Myanmar's total perimeter of 1,930 kilometres forms an uninterrupted coastline having the Andaman Sea to the south, and the Bay of Bengal to the southwest. The Union of Myanmar has a diverse population composition with many ethnic groups which were continuously fighting with the central authorities. The majority of the population is Burmans. It was part of the British Empire until 1948 and since then Myanmar continues to struggle to reduce its ethnic tensions.

The country's culture is heavily influenced by its neighbours and is based on a unique form of Buddhism intertwined with local customs and culture. Since the time of independence from Britain in January 1948, Myanmar has existed in a state of war with itself. Six decades of conflict have inflicted an enormous cost on the ethnic minorities. The continuous state of civil war has been marked by prolonged control by the country's armed forces for 50 of its 70 years of existence. The military *junta*, as it is generally referred to, ruled Myanmar with an iron fist and dominated every aspect of society including politics and the economy. A massive expansion of the armed forces (also referred to as *Tatmadaw*) between 1989 and 1995 helped the regime negotiate to ceasefire agreements with many of the ethnic insurgent groups who had been fighting it for decades. There has been large-scale violence and merciless repression. There is a possibility that the regime will simply crumble under its own weight through its failure to consolidate its control of the outlying areas of the country.

The British granted independence to Burma in 1948. Aung San, a hero of the country's struggle for independence, was unanimously elected the leader. However he was assassinated in the same year, and his colleague in the freedom struggle, U Nu, became the President. Nu was not a strong leader. The first signs of civil unrest erupted in 1958. Nu's refusal to grant semi-autonomy to the Shans and the Kayins prompted another rebellion in 1962 when General Ne Win imprisoned Nu and declared the setting up of the Tatmadaw or military government. Nu was released in 1966 and fled the country to organise a rebellion. His forces managed to hold some land in 1971, but they were eventually thrown out. In 1981, Ne Win stepped down, granting amnesty to all political enemies.

The two decades of the 1970s and 1980s saw a severe economic slowdown and rise in unemployment. In 1988, a huge demonstration led by students resulted in a violent crackdown by the *Tatmadaw*. Despite multi-party elections in 1990 that resulted in the main opposition party, the National League for Democracy, coming to power, key opposition leader and Nobel Peace Prize recipient Aung San Suu Kyi was placed under house arrest from 1989 to 1995 and again placed under house detention in September 2000. She was released after 19 months on 6 May 2002 and arrested again on 30 May 2003. Since then, the house arrest has been regularly extended. Suu Kyi continued to lead the movement but her supporters are routinely harassed or jailed.

The post-1990 era was the darkest period of the country's history with innumerable cases of human rights violations. Once it was clear that the people will be deprived of their democratic rights and that military rule would stay for more years, a number of countries (EU, USA and Canada) enforced economic and cultural sanctions. In 2008, a fresh constitution was formed which gave tremendous powers to the military. As per the new constitution, only 75 per cent of the seats for parliament would be available for elections and the remaining 25 per cent would be nominated by the commander-in-chief of the *Tatmadaw*.

Concurrently, whilst Myanmar was cut off from the rest of the world, China came to its rescue. In spite of serious ideological differences in the initial decades due to the presence of Communist party activities, which were subsequently banned by Myanmar, the decades following 1990 saw both the countries establishing strong trade and strategic relationships. The reasons for this proximity have been described by many analysts as a 'marriage of convenience.' Myanmar, at that time, was not only in need of military hardware but also an ally who could protect its interests while China, for its part, was looking at its strategic priorities and economic engagement. However, in 2007, when China thwarted the UN resolution in UNSC against Myanmar, the world for the first time openly witnessed the warm 'embrace'. Soon after this, China bagged the coveted 1400 kilometre oil and gas pipeline from the Bay of Bengal to underdeveloped Yunnan province. In the last 20 years, Chinese investment grew from a meagre $2 billion to 14.4 billion. This was a real watershed in their bilateral relations.

After the 2011 elections, the scenario changed. The new government of Thein Sein commenced political and economic reforms which opened the market to foreign investment, mainly from the West.

Observers had also commented that Myanmar's proximity to China was adversely affecting its international standing. In other words, failure to change its posturing from pro-China to pro-West would have prolonged Myanmar's international isolation and increased its dependence on China. The unprecedented support which Myanmar's nascent democratic government received from India, Japan, Europe and the USA not only bewildered China but Myanmar itself. The Westerly tilt by Myanmar's military *junta* to benevolent aid packages could not be set aside by any regime especially that is battling with a very weak economy.

In order to study the China-Myanmar conundrum, it is imperative to analyse the dependencies created between both of them, what is the attitude of the state and the people and how comfortable will be the Chinese regimes with the pro-democracy reforms being implemented and the patience of China to accept Western players to compete with it in the emerging markets. The growing proximity of the last two decades was watched very closely by Myanmar's neighbours, especially India. Of paramount interest to India was the growing military ties and establishment of electronic surveillance in the Indian Ocean very close to the Indian maritime boundary. However, in the last few years, the USA, Japan and EU have relaxed the sanctions and are willing to re-establish ties with the government of Myanmar.

Ancient Period

The history of Burma, now officially Myanmar, is long and complicated. Several ethnic groups have lived in the region, the oldest of which are probably the Mon or the Pyu. Some time in the first few centuries before Christ, the Mons found their way out of Central Asia and moved down to the Salween and Sittoung rivers. They spoke a dialect of the Mon-Khmer family of languages and were the first people known to inhabit what is now Myanmar. The Mons called the region the 'land of gold', practised Buddhism, and traded with India's great king, Ashoka. A few centuries later, the Pyus arrived from Tibet and they were followed by the Bamars who settled along the rich

Irrawaddy river, which they controlled from Pagan. The Bamars established the first Myanmar empire under King Anawrata. The Mons later rebelled but were quickly crushed by Kyanzitta, a Bamar general who soon became the ruler.

Kyanzitta's rise marked the beginning of Burma's golden age, when the bounty of rice irrigated by the Irrawaddy nourished the civilization. Thousands of temples were built and the arts flourished. However, within a century, the Mongols invaded the area and the kingdom was lost to them in 1287 at the battle of Vochan. The Mons and the Bamar withdrew to the south where they founded the enchanting city of Bago. In the north, descendants of the Tais, called the Shan, founded a kingdom at Innwa. Soon, the Mons and the Shans went to war at almost the same time when the Europeans began moving into Asia.

The Colonial Period

The Portuguese made the first inroads into Myanmar with a trade agreement with the Viceroy of Martaban in 1519. Along with the French and Dutch, the British set up colonies in Myanmar by the mid-seventeenth century. The British invaded Burma in 1819, conquering Rakhine, Tanintharyi, Assam and Manipur. During the 19th century, however, Burma became entangled in a competition for regional influence between the British and the French. Between 1824 and 1885, Burma fought three unsuccessful wars with the British, each of which resulted in the annexation of parts of the country to British India. When the capital of Mandalay finally fell, King Thibaw was exiled to India and the old political system was destroyed

In three short wars between 1824 and 1885, Burma was annexed into the British empire, not as a sovereign nation but as a province of India. The third Anglo-Burmese War in 1885 lasted for less than two weeks which resulted in the British taking over Mandalay. Mandalay was made the capital of northern Myanmar in 1857. The outmatched royal troops had surrendered quickly, although armed resistance in small pockets continued for several years. The people of Myanmar thought that the sole aim was to remove King Thibaw. But the British monarchy finally decided not only to annex all of northern Myanmar but to make the whole country a province of India with effect from January 1, 1886. Rangoon (now Yangon) was made the capital of this province. The loss of independence was painful enough; worse still was the British decision to eliminate the monarchy, in the process sending Thibaw into exile and to detach the government from religious affairs thus depriving the Buddhist monks of their traditional status and official patronage. Moreover, the British eliminated the office of the patriarch of the Buddhist clergy. The demise of the monarchy and the monkhood, the twin pillars of the society of Myanmar, was perhaps the most devastating aspect of the colonial period.

Many refused to accept the British victory and resorted to guerrilla warfare against the British army of occupation. The guerrillas were led mainly by former officers of the disbanded Royal Army, former officials (including village headmen) and royal princes and they considered themselves to be royal soldiers still fighting the Third Anglo-Burmese War. For the British, however, the war had ended legally with the annexation of the kingdom; those opposing them, therefore, were considered rebels and bandits.

For the next few years the British military officers acted as both judge and jury in dealing with captured guerrillas. Villagers who aided the rebels were also sternly punished. As the guerrillas fought on, the British adopted a 'strategic hamlet' strategy, whereby villages were burned and families and headmen uprooted from their homes and sent away to Lower Burma (which had been under British control since the Second Anglo-Burmese War). Strangers loyal to the colonial government were appointed as headmen for the new villages established by the British. The guerrillas resorted to desperate measures against the new village officials. By 1890, however, with more than 30,000 British and Indian troops engaged in the campaign, the military part of the struggle was over.

The Emergence of Nationalism

Those Burmese who attended the new schools established by the colonial government or by missionaries managed to gain admission to the clerical grades of government service, but even in those lower grades they encountered competition from Indians. Because science courses were not available, the professions of engineering and medicine were closed to the Burmese. Those who advanced to the government liberal arts college at Rangoon entered the middle grades of the civil service while a few went on to London to study law. When these young barristers returned to Burma, they were looked upon by the people as their new leaders. Their experience in the open environment of London had convinced these new leaders that some measure of political independence could be regained by negotiation.

The new leaders first turned their attention to the national religion, culture and education. In 1906, they founded the Young Men's Buddhist Association (YMBA) and through it began establishing a number of schools supported by private donations and government grants-in-aid (the YMBA was not anti-government). Three years later, the British, attempting to pacify the Indian National Congress, a broad-based and nationalist political party of India, introduced some constitutional reforms in India. Only a few minor changes were made in the Burmese constitution but these confirmed the young leaders' faith in British liberalism. In 1920, however, when it was learned that Burma would be excluded from the new reforms introduced in India, the barristers led the people in a countrywide protest that involved the boycott of British goods.

In 1920, Rangoon College was given the status of a full university by the University Act. However, the changes in the school's administration and curriculum were viewed as elitist and exclusionary of the Burmese population and its students went on strike. Younger school children followed them. The general public and the Buddhist clergy gave full support to this movement. The strikers camped in the courtyards of monasteries reviving memories of days when education was the concern of the monks. The University Act eventually was amended and the strike settled, but many strikers initially refused to go back to mission and government schools. The YMBA schools, now calling themselves 'national' schools, opened their doors to the strikers.

Constitutional reforms were finally granted in 1923, but the delay had split the leaders, some of whom, like the masses were beginning to doubt whether political freedom could be attained by peaceful protest. At the University of Rangoon itself, students began to resent their British professors. A radical student group began organizing protests, which came to be known as the *Thakin* movement. The name of this movement was purposely ironic: the Burmese word *thakin* ('master') was the term that the Burmese were required to use when addressing the British. In the 1930s, Burmese peasants, under the leadership of Saya San, rose in rebellion. Armed with only swords and sticks, they resisted British and Indian troops for two years. The young *Thakins*, though not involved in the rebellion, won the trust of the villagers and emerged as leaders in place of the British-educated Burmese elite.

In 1936, university students again went on strike, and two of their leaders, *Thakin* Nu (later called U Nu) and Aung San, joined the *Thakin* movement. In 1937, the British government separated Burma from India and granted it its own constitution, independent of that of India; the masses interpreted this as proof that the British planned to exclude Burma from the next phase of Indian reforms.

When World War II erupted in 1939, the Burmese leaders wanted to bargain with the government before extending their support to the British. A warrant was issued for the arrest of Aung San, but he escaped to China where he attempted to solicit support from radical groups. Assistance came instead from the Japanese government. Aung San returned to Burma secretly, recruited 29 young men and took them to Japan, where these 'Thirty Comrades' (including Ne Win, who later became head of state) received military training. The Japanese promised independence for Burma; hence, when Japanese troops reached Bangkok in December 1941, Aung San announced the formation of the Burma Independence Army (BIA). The Japanese advanced into Burma and by the end of 1942 had occupied the country. They subsequently disbanded the BIA and formed a smaller Burma Defence Army (BDA), with Aung San still as commander. Meanwhile, Thailand was given territory in the Shan states for its support of

Japan's wartime efforts; those lands were returned to Burma in the post-war period.

Ba Maw, the first prime minister under the 1937 constitution and later the leader of the opposition, was appointed head of state by the Japanese with a cabinet including Aung San and Thakin Nu. In 1943, when the tide of battle began to turn against them, the Japanese declared Burma a fully sovereign state. The Burmese government, however, was still a mere facade, with the Japanese army ruling. Meanwhile, Aung San had contacted Lord Louis Mountbatten, the Allied commander in Southeast Asia, as early as October 1943 to offer his cooperation, and in March 1945 Aung San and his army—renamed as the Burma National Army (BNA)—joined the British.

During the war Aung San and the *Thakins* formed a coalition of political parties called the Anti-Fascist Organization—renamed the Anti-Fascist People's Freedom League (AFPFL) after the war—which had wide popular support. After the defeat of the Japanese in Burma in May 1945, the British military administration and members of the pre-war government who had returned from exile demanded that Aung San be tried as a traitor. Mountbatten, however, recognized the extent of Aung San's hold on the BNA and on the general populace and he hastily sent the more conciliatory Sir Hubert Rance to head the administration. Rance regained for the British the trust of Aung San and the general public. When the war ended, the military administration was withdrawn and Rance was replaced by the former civilian governor who formed a cabinet consisting of older and more conservative politicians. The new administration arrested Aung San and charged him with treason. Surprised and angered, the Burmese people prepared for rebellion, but the British government in London wisely reinstated Rance who had proven himself a sensitive and successful administrator in Burma, as governor.

Rance formed a new cabinet, including Aung San, and discussions for a peaceful transfer of power began. These were concluded in London in January 1947 when the British agreed to Burma's independence. By June, the Burmese had decided to leave the British Commonwealth of Nations.

The communist and conservative wings of the AFPFL were dissatisfied with the agreement. The communists broke away and went underground and the conservatives went into opposition. In July, Aung San and most members of his cabinet were assassinated by gunmen sent by U Saw, a former prime minister and now a conservative. Rance asked Thakin Nu to form a new cabinet. A new constitution was written, and on January 4, 1948, Burma became a sovereign, independent republic.

Panglong Conference

On 12 February 1947, the Union of Burma was founded at the Panglong Conference by four former British colonies; these were primarily the Chin Hills, the Kachin Hills, the Federated Shan States and Burma Proper, all of which already had their own constitutions.

The British had occupied these four colonies separately as independent nations in different periods of time and had applied different administrative systems in accordance with the different constitutions that the colonial power had promulgated for them. The British officially promulgated the Chinram Constitution, called the 'Chin Hills Regulation,' in 1896, the 'Kachin Hill Tribes Regulation' in 1895, the '1919 Act of Federated Shan States' in 1920, and the '1935 Burma Act' in 1937. The Chin Hills Regulation of 1896 covered the present Chin State in Burma, the present Mizoram State, Nagaland State and part of Manipur and Meghalaya states in India. The 1935 Burma Act was applied to the area of the pre-colonial Myanmar/ Burman kingdom, which included the former Arakan and Mon kingdoms as well as the delta areas of Karen country.

The 1947 Panglong Conference, thus, was organized by the pre-colonial independent peoples and nations who, in principle, had had the right to regain their independence separately from Great Britain and to form their own respective nation-states or to remain as a British colony, or collectively reclaim their independence and found a new nation-state together. As mentioned in the preamble of the Panglong Agreement, they all opted for the third option which read: 'Believing that freedom will be more speedily achieved by the Shans, the Kachins and the Chins by their immediate co-operation with the interim Burmese government.'

The Panglong Agreement therefore represented a joint vision of the future of the pre-colonial independent people, namely, the Chin, Kachin, Shan and the interim Burmese government led by Chief Minister Aung San who came to power in August 1946 according to the Burma Act of 1935. The interim Burmese government was for the region formerly known as Burma Proper or Ministerial Burma, which included such non-Burman nationalities as the Mon, Rakhine (Arakan), and Karen. The Arakan and Mon were included because they were occupied by the British not as independent peoples but as the subjects of the kingdom of Burma.

The Karens were included in the Legislative Council of Ministerial Burma according to the 1935 Burma Act because the majority of them (more than two-thirds of the population) were living in delta areas side by side with the Burmans. Since these peoples were included in the legislative council of Ministerial Burma, Aung San could represent them in Panglong as the head of their government. Thus, the Panglong Agreement should be viewed as an agreement to found a new sovereign, independent nation-state between peoples from pre-colonial independent nations of what they then called Frontier areas (Chin Hills and Kachin Hills), Federated Shan State and Burma Proper, who in principle had the right to regain their independence directly from Great Britain and to form their own respective nation-states. In other words, the Panglong Agreement was an agreement signed between the peoples of a post-colonial nation-state-to-be.

The essence of the 'Panglong Agreement,', declared in its Preamble, was not only to hasten the ethnic peoples search for freedom but also to establish a new multi-national state of the Union of Burma for those who had struggled to free themselves from colonial power. Therefore, based on the 'Panglong Agreement.', the Constituent Assembly of the Interim Government of the Union of Burma promulgated a new constitution on September 24, 1947, thus paving the way for securing independence from Great Britain on January 4, 1948. Since the day on which the Union of Burma gained independence in 1948, which was also the same date the Panglong Agreement was signed, has been celebrated as Union Day. The observance of February 12 as Union Day means the mutual recognition of the Chin, Kachin, Shan and other nationalities, including the Burmans, as "different people historically and traditionally due to their differences in their language as well as cultural life." It is also a recognition of the distinct national identity of the Chin, Kachin, Shan and other nationalities that had the right to gain their own independence separately and to set up their own nation-state separately. In other words, it is the recognition of the pre-colonial independent status of the Chin, Kachin and Shan and other nationalities as well as their post-colonial status of nation-state-to-be.

Period of Unsettled Democracy

Myanmar was granted independence on 4 January 1948 by the efforts of revolutionary leader Gen Aung San who is known as 'The Father of the country." Aung San was assassinated shortly after independence and Myanmar was subsequently led by prime minister U Nu. Civilian rule lasted until 1962, except for a brief period between 1958 and 1960. All the while, the government was trying to deal with insurgencies in the countryside.

The Communist Party of Burma (CPB) began an armed insurrection in March 1948, the KNU in January 1949 and armed conict rapidly spread among other ethnic groups, including the Karenni, Mon, Pao, Rakhine, and Muslims of north Arakan. Dozens of towns across the country fell to insurgent forces and at one stage the authority of prime minister U Nu's government extended barely six miles from Yangon, the capital. Gradually, central government authority was restored and the Burmese armed forces, known as the *Tatmadaw*, was rebuilt by the new military chief, General Ne Win, using troops from his old unit, the 4th Burma Ries. However, throughout the 1950s, much of the countryside and many ethnic minority regions remained under the control of insurgent groups. During this turbulent times, the difficulties of the government were further compounded by the invasion of several thousand Kuomintang (KMT) troops into the Shan state after the communist victory in China. Critically, it was the KMT incomers who elevated the illicit opium trade to international proportions. Nevertheless, in government-controlled areas, parliamentary government continued and, during 1958, a number of cease-re agreements were reached with Mon, Pao, Rakhine and communist forces under U Nu's 'arms for democracy' initiative. All the time the institutional strength of Ne Win's *Tatmadaw* was growing. In particular, many senior officers were increasingly critical of what they saw as the failure of the politicians to overcome factionalism in government and insurgency in the field.

By 1958, Burma was well on the road to internal peace and economic recovery but the ruling AFPFL had become divided by personal quarrels between U Nu and his closest associates. Amid rumours of a military takeover, U Nu invited the army chief of staff, Ne Win, who had been a *Thakin* with him, one of the Thirty Comrades, and Aung San's second in command—to assume the premiership. This move sometimes has been called a 'constitutional coup'. Ne Win established internal security, stabilized the military position and prepared the country for general elections which took place in February 1960.

U Nu was returned to office with an absolute majority. In 1961, he attempted to legislate Buddhism as Burma's state religion, only to raise tensions among Christians in the Kachin state where a new insurgent movement was getting under way. In the Shan state too armed movements were forming as the younger generation grew increasingly impatient. The government of U Nu was unable to cope with the insurgencies.

Burmese Way of Socialism

In March 1962, the Army Chief Ne Win led a military coup and arrested U Nu, the chief justice and several cabinet ministers. He justified his action as a means of keeping the Union from disintegrating. Suspending the 1947 constitution, which had been in effect since independence, he ruled the country with a Revolutionary Council consisting of senior military officers. Ne Win's stated purpose was to make Burma a truly socialist state. A military-controlled one-party Burma Socialist Programme Party (BSPP) system was established. Following unsuccessful peace talks with most of the different armed opposition groups in 1963-1964, Ne Win then embarked on his 26-year experiment with the 'Burmese Way to Socialism.' Abandoning Aung San's 'Unity in Diversity' and the federal structure of the 1947 constitution, he adopted a two-fold strategy: to run an all-out counter-insurgency campaign in the rural countryside while at the same time trying to establish a centralised, one-party system of government radiating from Rangoon into the ethnic minority states. As a result, many serious human rights violations such as the enforced conscription of civilian labourers and forcible relocation were first systematised under the Burma Socialist Programme Party government of General Ne Win. These measures did not improve the economy, however, particularly as investment in agriculture was generally sacrificed in favour of industrial growth, and the military replaced civilians in key administrative positions.

Ne Win had promised a new constitution and in September 1971 representatives of the party's central committee with the country's various ethnic groups and of other interest groups were appointed to draft a document. A referendum to ratify the new constitution was held in December 1973 with more than 90 percent of eligible voters signifying approval; the constitution was promulgated in January 1974. Elections to the People's Assembly (Pyithu Hluttaw)—the supreme legislative, executive and judicial authority—and to local People's Councils were held early in 1974; the new government took office in March with Ne Win as president.

After the establishment of the new political organization, Burma's economy grew steadily at a moderate pace. A notable policy change was a partial relaxation of the ban on foreign financial aid and considerable funding was received from the Asian Development Bank and the International Bank for Reconstruction and Development (part of the World Bank) as well as from Japan. By the early 1980s, however, growth was being increasingly hindered by mounting trade deficits

'Unity in Diversity' vs. 'Burmese Way to Socialism'

Two home-grown philosophies have dominated Burma's political life over the last 50 years: Aung San's 'Unity in Diversity', and Ne Win's 'Burmese Way to Socialism'. In his Blueprint for a Free Burma, Aung San combined a mixture of nationalist, communist and parliamentary ideas. He called for equal economic development and simultaneous independence for all ethnic groups as the best way to bring the country together. However, although he publicly recognized the historic independence of several minority groups, he believed only the Shans could be properly classified as a 'nation'. Other groups would receive only varying degrees of regional autonomy to qualify for full 'national minority' rights. He followed Stalin in suggesting that they should form at least ten per cent of the population. Although Aung San was the founder of the modern Burmese army, the *Tatmadaw*, he believed in civilian government and resigned from the army to enter politics. Ne Win, in contrast, believed that the military was the only institution which could hold such an ethnically diverse country together. A whimsical blend of Buddhist, Marxist and nationalist principles, the unitary philosophy of his 'Burmese Way to Socialism' was never elaborated on from a short text, The System of Correlation of Man and his Environment. Under the 1974 constitution, there were clear guarantees for the basic rights of all citizens 'regardless of race, religion, status or sex'. But a 'socialist society' was declared the goal of the state, under a rigid one party system.

caused largely by falling commodity export prices, increasing costs of imports and rising external debt payments. A series of economic reforms proposed in 1987–1988 was intended to reverse the socialist policies enacted in the early 1960s. Chief among these were the active encouragement of foreign investment and a considerable liberalization of foreign trade.

Communist and ethnic insurgencies had expanded in the eastern and northern parts of the country throughout the BSPP period. In May 1980, Ne Win offered full amnesty to all political insurgents inside or outside Burma who reported to authorities within a 90-day period. Most notable among those accepting the offer was U Nu, who, after having gone into exile in India in 1969, returned to enter a Buddhist monastery. Most insurgents, however, chose to continue opposing the government, and repeated attempts by government troops to suppress them met with only limited success. After four decades, insurgency had become a way of life.

Under General Ne Win, Burma disappeared behind a bamboo curtain as the door to the outside world was rmly closed. Indeed, in 1979, Ne Win even withdrew Burma from the Non-Aligned Movement. Within the country, however, he sought to rearrange politics completely under a monolithic system of one-party rule. Since the days of the independence struggle, most political movements in Burma stood at the left-of-centre and Ne Win's rhetorical ideas also appeared driven by competition with the CPB and Mao Zedong's communist government in China where he had visited in 1960. But his political vision, the 'Burmese Way to Socialism,' was always lightly sketched. For 26 years, Ne Win pursued a basic two-fold strategy: on the one hand, attempting to build up the centralized control of the Burma Socialist Programme Party (BSPP), while, on the other, launching an all-out offensive against insurgent groups in the countryside. In contrast to the pluralism of the 1947 Constitution, priority was now given to a socialist and Burmese national identity, shared by all ethnic groups.

Only at the beginning did he appear to hesitate during peace talks with insurgent groups in 1963–1964. Following their failure, he cracked down on the entire opposition. Hundreds of political opponents were arrested, the economy was nationalized, foreigners and missionaries expelled and all independent media and schools taken over. Tight security controls were also placed on students, Buddhist monks and other religious groups as every sector of society came under the control of the central government and the Military Intelligence Service. Under the 1974 Constitution, an attempt was made to systematize the BSPP administration of Burma. Seven ethnic minority states were drawn up with the addition of new Chin, Mon and Rakhine (Arakan) states. They thus equalled in number the seven 'divisions' where ethnic Burmans were in a majority. There were also guarantees for the basic rights of all citizens before the law 'regardless of race, religion, status or sex' (Article 22), but many minorities believed that the 'Burmese Way to Socialism' was simply a cloak for 'Burmanization' in a new political guise. With the closure of independent and religious-based schools, minority languages virtually disappeared beyond fourth grade in education and publications in non-Burmese languages which had ourished in the 1950s, were severely restricted under the 1962 printers and publishers Registration Law. Equally criticized, the ethnic minorities were increasingly excluded from senior levels in the *Tatmadaw* and government. In effect, to participate in BSPP leadership meant suppressing their non-Burman identities. In an echo of the communal tensions of the 1930s, a new xenophobia was also apparent. This time it appeared to be officially endorsed, evidenced by the exodus of around 100,000 Indians and 100,000 Chinese—many of whom were inuential in business—during the economic nationalization programmes that began in 1963–64.

Eventually, in mid-1967, quite a few Chinese were reportedly killed in anti-Chinese riots that spread from Rangoon; this led to a complete breakdown in relations with neighbouring China. At that time, however, most concerns were expressed about a new ruthlessness on the battleeld. Especially notorious was a counter-insurgency campaign, known as the 'Four Cuts' (*hpyat lei-byat*), which was modelled on the US 'strategic hamlet' operations in Vietnam. Under this programme, large areas were declared 'free-re' zones and villagers were ordered to move into defended settlements under government control. Anyone attempting to remain in the homes risked being shot on sight. First introduced in the Irrawaddy delta region in the late 1960s, this tactic was successively introduced into other areas of the country over the next two decades, further exacerbating the internal displacement of civilians that had begun in 1948–1949.

Far from ending resistance, such heavy-handed tactics saw a marked revival of insurgency. Two additional factors now escalated the state of conict which threatened to bring in international actors as well. First, following the anti-Chinese riots in 1967, the People's Republic of China began a decade of full-scale military backing of the CPB, which was able to seize control of much of the north-east borderlands, mainly in the Shan state. As Ne Win's rule became ever more idiosyncratic, it was against this bleak backdrop that, in the mid-1980s, the Burmese economy inched to the brink of international bankruptcy. In a country with no external military engagements, over 40 per cent of the national budget was being spent on military activities. With student protests escalating, in July 1988, Ne Win suddenly resigned. His military socialist vision was on the brink of collapse.

1988 and Beyond

The '8888' uprising refers to a series of protests that took place in Burma during 1988 that culminated on the date 8/8/1988, giving the uprising its name. These protests, which began in March 1988, were initially incited largely by students to express their disgust with the military government's hostile economic, political and monetary policies. The one-party rule led by the Burmese Socialist Program Party (BSPP) suppressed the democratic desires of the people and the economic situation in Burma placed it on the 'Least Developed Country' list of the United Nations Economic and Social Council by 1987. The government at that time was headed by General Ne Win who ruled Burma from 1962 to 1988 as an oppressive and violent ruler. Despite Ne Win's resignation in July 1988, the protests and anger continued since his successor, Sein Lwin, was also hated by the Burmese and he refused to address the issues that the protesters were calling for action on.

Although the centre of the uprising was in the Burmese capital city of Rangoon, the rural areas also witnessed scenes of protests and strikes. From August 1 to 7 of that year, the protests intensified as students called upon everyone to get involved and participate in the mass demonstration planned for August 8. The people responded and the streets were filled with monks, workers, intellectuals and members of all ethnic groups and from all walks of life. The August 8 demonstration stretched into a five-day strike that took the Burmese military government by surprise. This was followed with promises from the leadership that the people's demands would be considered although, of course, these promises were never meant to be fulfilled. Rather, during this time, it is estimated that around 3,000 people were killed as the police and military massacred peaceful protestors under orders from the BSPP. With the surprise resignation of Sein Lwin on August 12, the protests only paused for a few days before resuming again with increased violence as the Burmese people fought for their rights and the regime stepped up its repression. This was towards the end of August when Aung San Suu Kyi first entered the political arena with an address to the masses of people gathered at Shwedagon pagoda in Rangoon. She instantly became a symbol of democracy and freedom for the Burmese people. In September, 75 per cent of the delegates voted for a multi-party system but the BSPP rejected any change. The rioting continued and members of the army and police forces began to side with the protesters. Finally, on September 18, 1988, the Burmese military again took over the government and quickly suppressed the protests using extremely violent measures. Led by General Saw Maung, the 1974 constitution was repealed and martial law instituted with the establishment of the 'State Law and Order Restoration Council (SLORC).'

Many believed that had the United Nations or the USA had become involved during these protests or refused to recognize the coup during its takeover, the military regime would have failed to take hold and would have collapsed. To commemorate the bloody '8888' uprising, groups around the world have been holding remembrance meetings every year on August 8 since then.

3

MYANMAR'S GEOSTRATEGIC IMPORTANCE FOR INDIA AND CHINA

Geostrategic Importance of Myanmar

Myanmar occupies a critical geostrategic position in the Asian continent. It is a meeting point between South Asia and South East Asia. It is sandwiched between two Asian giants—China, with which it shares long land borders and India with which it shares land as well as maritime boundaries. Both sides of the borders have hamlets of rebellious ethnic groups and independent armies which are continuously struggling with the government. In the first and second world wars, Burma's strategic location was well used by the British and later by the Japanese. Myanmar's strategic importance substantially reduced after 1962 when the country was taken over by a military-backed government which kept the country in self-imposed isolation. However, after 1988, the country returned to the limelight with China and India both vying to use its vital geostrategic location. This location gives it a strategic significance of powerful implications for China and India. It also shares a long border with Laos and Thailand. Its extended seaboard providing the eastern flank to the Bay of Bengal is of critical naval significance to India.

With 667,000 square kilometres, Myanmar is the largest

independent state in mainland Southeast Asia. Its 5,876-kilometre land boundary touches five different countries including two strategic giants. To the west, it shares a 1,463 kilometre border with India, a nuclear power that dominates the South Asian subcontinent and the Bay of Bengal. To the northeast, Burma shares a 2,185 kilometre-long border with China, now within reach of a great power status. In the east, Burma's frontier runs southwest and south for 1,800 kilometres alongside Thailand, which is an influential player in the sub-region and ASEAN. At its eastern-most point, Burma shares a short border with Laos (235 kilometres) and at its western-most point with Bangladesh (193 kilometres). While in most of the borders the terrain is rugged and heavily forested, they have always been porous to the local people and replete with drug smugglers, insurgents, ethnic groups and traders.

Burma's coastline is 1,930 kilometres long, not counting the 852 islands that lie within its waters, mostly in the Mergui Archipelago. Burma faces the Bay of Bengal west of the capital, Naypyidaw and the Andaman Sea to the south. The Burmese government declared a territorial sea of 12 nautical miles (22 kilometres) and a zone of 24 nautical miles (44 kilometres). Since then, Burma has also laid claim to a continental shelf and an exclusive economic zone (EEZ) of 200 nautical miles (370 kilometres), thus extending its maritime interests to cover an area of 148,600 square kilometres. While Myanmar's security concerns have mostly been land-based, the large stretch of open ocean and coastal waters has been used by local fishermen, traders, smugglers and the navies of other countries. Myanmar's location does not dominate any major sea lanes of communication (SLOC); however it is criss-crossed by a number of important east-west commercial air routes.

A major dispute over the land boundary with China was satisfactorily resolved in 1960 and the land border with Bangladesh was agreed to in 1999, but differences over territorial claims still arise with Myanmar's neighbours. These disputes tend to occur as a result of poorly demarcated boundaries and shifting river courses leading to occasional tensions with Thailand in particular.

Maritime disputes are also common. Burma has laid claim to its waters in a number of ways that seem to violate the United Nations Convention on the Law of the Sea. An agreement was reached with India over some of Burma's claims in 1986 and in 1993 a trilateral agreement was negotiated between Burma, India and Thailand over the trijunction point between the three countries in the Andaman Sea. However, Myanmar has yet to settle a number of maritime disputes with Thailand and Bangladesh, which still cause problems over fishing rights. Myanmar has also attracted criticism from the USA for some of its broader claims, including its insistence that foreign warships must obtain permission from Naypyitaw prior to entering its territorial waters and contiguous zone.

Terrain Analysis

Surrounded by rugged mountains to the west, north, and east, and wide seas in the south, Myanmar is to a large extent geographically self-contained. Communications with the rest of the world are poor. Indeed, before 1938, there were no road or rail routes to any neighbouring countries. The Second World War saw the construction of the Burma Road between Chungking and Lashio, the Ledo Road from Mogaung to Ledo in north eastern Assam and a railway line from Ban Pong in Thailand through Three Pagodas Pass to Thanbyuzayat. Access to Burma overland is still very restricted, but there are projects under way to restore parts of the old Burma and Ledo Roads and to upgrade land communications with India and Thailand. There are still no international rail links, but it is possible that the old Japanese line from Thailand may eventually be rebuilt as part of a proposed trans-Asia railway.

As a result of all these factors, most legitimate foreign trade over the last many centuries has been through the sea route. This is not to discount the massive scale of smuggling across Myanmar's land borders since 1962, a problem that has hardly been solved by a 1989 agreement legalizing border trade with China and in 1996 with India.

Within Myanmar, most rivers run north to south, as also main road and rail corridors. East-west travel is difficult. Burma boasts of a massive 12,800 kilometres of inland waterways, 3,200 kilometres of which are navigable by large commercial vessels. The Irrawaddy river, permits traffic to penetrate from the sea to Bhamo, more than 1,000 kilometres inland and only 50 kilometres from the Chinese border. The Sittang, lower Chindwin and lower Salween rivers are also used extensively by launches and other river boats, as is the maze of distributaries and creeks in the Irrawaddy delta. Because of this, the role of river navigation in traditional rural life is extensively used and these waterways remain the backbone of the country's transport network. Myanmar also has 28,200 kilometres of roads, but most people still follow the rivers and railway corridors. Ironically only 3,440 kilometres of roads are paved. Since Independence, Myanmar has placed increasing reliance on air transport but the national fleet has always been small. Of the country's 80 airfields, only three have paved runways over 2,400 metres. Most are unpaved.

Myanmar's rulers have long been fearful of the massive populations of their larger neighbours and the potential threats they pose. The country's birth rate has been rising, but its population of 55 million is dwarfed by those of China and India, the world's two most-populous countries, with 1.5 billion and 1.2 billion people respectively. At an average of 73.5 people per square kilometre, Burma's population density is much lower than most major Southeast Asian countries. The demographic spread of population in the nation is not homogeneous. At present, about 68 per cent is made up of ethnic Burmans who have traditionally dominated the central lowlands. The remainder of the population is divided between numerous ethnic groups and subgroups, most of which have concentrated in separate areas around the country's mountainous periphery. The most important of these groups are the Shan (who constitute 9 per cent of the population), Karen (7 per cent), Arakanese (4 per cent) and Mon (2 per cent). There are significant groups of Chin, Kachin, Kayah (Karenni), Pao, Palaung, Lahu, Wa and Rohingya. There are also sizeable communities of Chinese (3 per cent of the population) and Indians (2 per cent), most of whom are found in the urban areas and along the main transport corridors.

Despite the development of a few cities like Yangon (with 4 million people), Mandalay (800,000) and Moulmein (300,000), about 70 per cent of Burma's population still lives in small rural towns and villages. Roughly the same proportion is dependent on agriculture as the main means of livelihood, a figure that has been surprisingly constant for the past century. Burma enjoys an abundance of natural resources, and has been described as potentially the richest country in Southeast Asia. Before the Second World War, it was the largest rice producer in the world and a major exporter of oil. Even now, about half the country remains covered by forests, its fishing grounds are relatively unexploited and it has 75 per cent of the world's reserves of teak.

Myanmar had not completely recovered from the aftermath of the second world war and the British granting it independence, when management of the economy fell into the hands of the armed forces which adopted an ideology known as the Burmese Way to Socialism. Despite some modest growth, this doctrine and highly centralized system was a manifest failure and in 1987 Myanmar was declared by the United Nations to be one of the world's least developed countries (LDC). Despite some improvement in the economy since 1988, largely due to a more open system, state enterprises remain highly inefficient and privatization efforts were stalled. There have been attempts to widen the economic base but the industrial sector is still a miniscule part of the economy. At USD 300, Myanmar's average annual per capita income is lower than most other Asia-Pacific countries. Nearly 25 per cent of the population is below the official United Nations designated poverty line.

With the economic fillip of China and India in the decade of the Nineties, the geostrategic importance of Myanmar has increased multifold in the South East Asia region. Both India and China see it as a potential pivot; India for ASEAN and China for access to the Indian Ocean and as an alternative route of pumping oil and reduce dependence on the Malacca Strait. In the process of redistribution of the power equation between China and the USA, Southeast Asian countries are playing an important role. Myanmar's location in Southeast Asia, as well as common land borders with China, makes it a viable land bridge to the Indian Ocean. Its coastline on the Bay of Bengal allows it to control the eastern Indian Ocean where major sea routes are located for oil transportation from Africa and the Middle East to China, Japan and South Korea.

Myanmar's Geostrategic importance for China

China's economic rise is associated with a high dependence on imported oil from Africa (Angola, Sudan) and the Middle East (Iran, Saudi Arabia) which is transported via sea routes in the Indian Ocean. It is a known fact that sea routes in coastal East and Southeast Asia are controlled by the USA. The presence of the Pacific Fleet is not a hidden fact. Of serious significance is the choke-point at Malacca Strait, a maritime bottleneck between Indonesia, Malaysia and Singapore. Malacca Strait is a 200-kilometre wide strait and the entry-exit points are controlled by the USA. If this is blocked oil tankers have to make an additional circuit of about 2000-kilometres. Should Washington, in case of a conflict with Beijing, block this strait, China would be cut off from its energy imports for a long time.

In this context, the strategic interest of China in Myanmar is clear: the country offers a transit corridor to the Indian Ocean, bypassing the Strait of Malacca. In 2013, two 1000-kilometre long pipelines connected the deep-water port of Kyaukphyu in Arakan State on the Bay of Bengal with Kunming in Yunnan/China. The oil from Africa and the Middle East and gas from the offshore seabed are transported across through Myanmar to China directly. To safeguard its maritime trade routes, China has created a chain of port bases along the Indian Ocean: Gwadar (Pakistan), Hambantota (Sri Lanka), Chittagong (Bangladesh) and Sittwe (Myanmar).

China's navy is also present: Chinese submarines patrol the international waters of Southeast Asia and in the Indian Ocean—near the Andamans and Nicobars, two groups of islands belonging to India.

Myanmar's Strategic Importance for India

Myanmar is geostrategically important for India too, as it is the only ASEAN country that shares a border with India. It is also the only country that can act as a link between India and ASEAN countries. Myanmar is India's gateway to Southeast Asia and could provide the required impetus to India's 'Look East' and 'Act East' policy. To this end, India has decided to upgrade the Kalewa-Yargyi road segment to a highway while Myanmar would develop the remaining part of the road, i.e., the Yargyi-Monywa portion, and this will connect Moreh in India to Mae Sot in Thailand via Myanmar. This, in turn, would improve India's long dream of connecting with both Myanmar and Thailand.

If India is to become an assertive regional player in Asia, it has to work towards developing policies that would improve and strengthen it domestically which will encourage more confidence in its ability to lead the region and be an important global player. Competition with China should also be considered and taken seriously. China's growing influence in the region would lead to a more one-sided dynamics in the region.

India, on the other hand, needs to use its soft power more effectively and at the same time strengthen itself domestically and regionally. China has used its soft power as well as through its trade and economic relations with Myanmar by taking up large infrastructure projects in the country.

There are several advantages that India has over China with regard to Myanmar. One is the democratic process, which results in different governments at the centre and states through free and fair elections. There is also the respect for institutions that are strong enough to hold the country together. Finally, cooperation in different multilateral forums such as ASEAN and BIMSTEC strengthen the relationship between the two countries. Besides, India has sent a clear signal that while economic ties are important, it is keen to build a holistic relationship and is prepared to assist in institution building in Myanmar. For this, a large number of Indian MNCs have already taken up projects in Myanmar. In December 2012, President Thein Sein came to India and addressed Indian industry barons to invest in Myanmar. Army chiefs of both the countries have also exchanged visits in the last three years and identified areas of mutual cooperation from the military point of view.

Implications of Geostrategic Importance for India and China

Until recently, Myanmar, the former British colony, had been within the sphere of China's interest, the country that to a great extent depends on oil supplies, especially from the Persian Gulf and African states going through the Indian Ocean. That is the route through which 50 per cent of world containerized shipping and 70 per cent of global oil products supplies pass. The Ocean is a risky part of the planet. There are 11 sea points along vital hydrocarbons supply routes of the world that are most vulnerable to possible closure. The major part of them is situated in the Indian Ocean. The energy factor was decisive while working out the 'String of Pearls' strategy. The term itself was invented by the experts of the US Army's Strategic Studies Institute and appeared in its publication 'String of Pearls: Meeting the Challenge of China's Rising Power Across the Asian Littoral' that saw light in 2006.

China's plans to protect its sea supply routes are seen as a direct challenge to US regional interests. Its strategy envisages the creation of footholds such as naval and air force facilities or friendly call ports stretching from the Chinese island of Hainan in the East to the Pakistani port of Gwadar in the West to guarantee secure and regular oil supplies to the mainland. Eighty-five per cent of oil and its products are supplied to China from the Persian Gulf and Africa across the Indian Ocean including the narrow Malacca Strait controlled by the USA and its regional allies. The area is subject to pirate attacks that are a threat to the sea lanes used for transport of hydrocarbons and other material to China. That is where the geostrategic importance of Myanmar comes to the fore. By strengthening its presence in Myanmar, China guarantees access to one of the most important strategic sea lanes in the world—the Malacca Strait. Beijing can go to any length to make the bilateral relations with Myanmar as close as it can. In May 2011, the President of Myanmar, Thein Sein, elevated the bilateral relationship by establishing a 'comprehensive strategic cooperative partnership.' Military cooperation is on the rise.

If China upgrades Myanmar's naval facilities it has access to the Indian Ocean and guarantee the southern neighbour's security, which becomes a win-win situation for both. The Chinese build shore-based radars maintenance and replenishment infrastructure, including the surveillance station on Coco Islands seem to be located with the primary aim to monitor the Malacca Strait and naval exercises conducted in the area.

2015 Election and the Present Day Scenario

The 2010 election which were boycotted by the main opposition party, the National League of Democracy (NLD), resulted in the formation of a quasi-military government by the military-backed Union Solidarity and Development Party (USDP). The then President, Thein Sein (an ex-General of the Myanmarese Military) not only promised human rights freedom but also started undertaking positive reforms. The NLD welcomed it and so did the Western world. Soon the Noble Laureate and icon of democracy in Myanmar, Aung San Suu Kyi, was invited the world over. At home too she was emerging as the leader of the masses. China which had established very close strategic and military ties with the military junta in the last two decades and had invested huge sums of money in Myanmar observed these developments very closely.

India on the other hand was an ardent pro-democracy supporter and aligned itself with Aung San Suu Kyi. However, seeing the influx of Chinese influence, India too, as part of its 'Look East Policy' started to engage with the military junta of Myanmar in the mid-Nineties. The positive political reform process by the Thein Sein government including release of hundreds of pro-democracy supporters and lifting of the ban on press and media, made USA, Europe and Japan lift the sanctions partly. The world hailed his efforts. However the country's 2008 constitution was so made that it gave sweeping powers to the military including 25 per cent of the seats in both houses of Parliament. Before the next election in 2015, the government promised a free and open process. Having settled that issue to rest, on 8 July 2015, Myanmar's Union Election Commission (UEC) declared that the general election will be held on 8 November 2015. Election 2015 in Myanmar is just the third after its independence in 1948. Hence, all eyes were glued to this historic election. Everybody was watching the developments in the nation very closely. The election was held on 8 November 2015 which was watched by even international observers including some politicians from Australia and New Zealand. The results were historic. The NLD led by Aung San Suu Kyi won a historic and landslide victory winning over 80 per cent of the contested seats in both houses of parliament. The new democratic government formed under the NLD has a herculean task at hand. It has not only to tackle the shattering economy but also work on removing poverty and uplifting education and infrastructure in many other sectors. Located on the crossroads of South and South East Asia, Myanmar will also have to balance between the two Asian powers and also the increasing interest of EU, Japan and USA which see it as a potential market. Which way will the new government tilt needs to be seen and analysed.

4

China–Myanmar Relations and Strategic Ties

Introduction

China and Myanmar share a long boundary and over the years have developed strong strategic and economic ties. After the 1990 coup by the Myanmar military, the USA and many Western countries had imposed economic and trade sanctions on Myanmar. During this time China kept its door open and within no time became the largest investor and trading partner of Myanmar. Though Myanmar participates in only a miniscule portion of China's total trade, when we study the intricacies of the relationship it was more of a symbiotic one at that time. An understanding of the past and present of the actions of China and Myanmar will enable a more concise view of their strategic relations. The future of Sino-Myanmar relations depends on the balance that China will establish between its economic development and international reputation on the one hand, and the strengthening of its relationship with Myanmar's new regime which was established in 2016 on the other. China-Myanmar relations, since diplomatic recognition in 1950 until today can be briefly divided into the following phases: first, ambivalent peaceful coexistence (1949-1961); second, temporary setback (1962-1970); third, improving relationship (1971-1988); fourth, closer ties from 1989 to 2010. The fourth phase saw the most significant change in Myanmar's China policy, that is, it shifted from 'strategic neutrality' to 'strategic alignment' after the coup, when the military junta took over power in 1988. The relationship and partnership after the restoration of complete democracy in 2016 is still in an ambiguous stage. The history of Sino-Myanmar relations is replete with tremendous turbulence. At the time of independence in 1948, Myanmar had a sizeable Chinese population which was generally engaged in private business.

After the 1962 military takeover, the BSPP established the 'Burmese Way of Socialism' under Gen Ne Win. Towards this end, in 1963-1964, there was a spate of economic nationalization programmes introduced in the country. This saw the closure of a large number of business houses. The apathy of the regime against private business houses resulted in large-scale exodus of Indian and Chinese origin persons who were affected severely. Some persons had estimated an exodus of about 1,00,000 Sino-Burmese nationals, many of whom were influential businessmen in Rangoon. This created a slight dent in the relations. Though the Ne Win regime decided to ignore, it, the worst was yet to come.

Influenced by the Cultural Revolution in China, the Chinese population in Rangoon started wearing Mao badges. This was in contravention of the local regulation and when some young Chinese were ordered to remove them, they resisted. As a result, anti-Chinese riots broke out in Rangoon on 26 June 1967. They erupted due to defiance shown by Chinese students of the Burmese government's ban on wearing Mao badges in school and this led to a deterioration of Sino–Burmese relations. According to some eyewitnesses, the police did not interfere in the looting and arson till the Chinese embassy was attacked by some locals. This incident was followed by withdrawal of the ambassadors of both the nations and also the expulsion of the *Xinhua* (New China News Agency) correspondent from Rangoon. Beijing immediately suspended its aid programme to Burma which it had started in 1960 under the Friendship Treaty. These riots contributed immensely to estranged relations between Beijing and Rangoon throughout the 1970s and 1980s. This period then saw

China coming out openly in support of the Communist Party of Burma (CPB), which till now was on its own and did not have much support in Myanmar. Chinese media started targeting the Ne Win government. Support to the CPB and aid continued to be an important aspect of Chinese foreign policy throughout the 1970s and stopped only after the death of Mao Zedong and change of leadership in China in 1976. Despite the normalization of bilateral ties in 1970, the relations did not really pick up post-1990, when the *Tatmadaw* (Myanmar military) desperately needed modernization. And the only country that could help it with its modernization programme was China as the West had isolated Myanmar diplomatically. Thus, the military regime did not blink at all in getting into trade and military ties. What is evident from the above discussion is that its proximity to China was the need of the hour for the embattled military government at that time. Besides, China and Myanmar also developed relations with Pakistan, India and other neighbouring states.

China's Interest in Myanmar

It is expected that China will seek to increase its influence in the region for the exploitation of Myanmar's natural resources. The possible obstacles to China's ambitions include border instability, growing resentment against the local Chinese population in Myanmar and stronger and new international players who could affect China's economic trade. China's relations with Myanmar are part of its 'Go West' campaign since 2000. It aims to eliminate poverty and bridge the economic gap between China's coastal and western provinces within the next 50 years. Between 1996 and 2005, the Myanmar-Yunnan border trade accounted for about 50 per cent of Myanmar's total trade value; nearly 80 per cent of its exports to China and about 40 per cent of Myanmar's imports go through border trade. The China-Myanmar border trade has flourished in recent years. China's exports increased 3.1 times, from US$ 261.2 million in 2001 to US$ 800 million in 2007, while China's imports increased 2.5 times from US$ 93.7 million in 2001 to US$ 231.6 million in 2007.

The 'Malacca Dilemma,' refers to China's excessive reliance on the strait with 60-70 per cent of its oil shipments passing through it. Two threats emerge from this: first, piracy and maritime terrorism; second, influence or dominance of other powers over the strait. China has increased its presence in the region by developing special diplomatic and strategic relations.

China's Access to Myanmar's Resources

China's interest in Myanmar ranges from mining and oil and gas to hydropower. To secure these resources, China will outbid all other players, build necessary infrastructure at a low cost, provide low-interest loans, arms and technical assistance, provide a political umbrella for the regime in the international community and maintain good bilateral relations with ethnic groups and the military government. In order to get access to Myanmar's natural resources, China is not afraid of paying the highest price. The resources are limited and China believes that their price can only increase. As known, the Chinese adopt a long-term perspective to secure any strategic resource rather than a short-term one.

It will be interesting to note that in 2003, China lost an oil agreement with Kazakhstan to a Western company that was already exploring the field. But two years later, China was again competing for oil in the same region. This time, rather than buying the rights to explore the oil fields, it proposed to buy a company and that too at a high price. By 2009, China owned a 67 per cent stake in the company Kazakhstan Inc. which produced around 200,000 barrels a day. It is believed that China paid $ 4.18 billion for the company, clearly showing its will to acquire the resources at any cost.

In 2005-2006, China demonstrated its diplomatic and business acumen when it signed an agreement with Myanmar to sell 6.25 trillion cubic feet of natural gas from A-1 to A-3 blocks (Rakhine coastline) through a pipeline that would connect Kunming in China's Yunnan province and the Myanmarese port of Kyaukphyu in Rakhine state for the next 30 years. This agreement came as a shock to Indian authorities who had spent several years negotiating with Myanmar for a Myanmar-Bangladesh-India pipeline.

Investment and Economic Assistance: China's investment and economic assistance in Myanmar is part of its 'Go Out' strategy. In practice, China has provided generous government support and preferential loans. In the last decade, Myanmar has received economic assistance in the form of grants, interest-free loans and concessional loans or debt reliefs.

According to the Asia Research Institute, China-Myanmar trade in 2005 was US$ 1209.25 million. Between 1989 and 2005, Myanmar's exports increased 2.2 times while its imports from China increased almost five times. During this period, China's FDI in Myanmar was only US$ 194.2 million. China gave economic assistance to protect its own investments and influenced the military government and ethnic groups to pursue economic trade with Myanmar.

Development and Financial Assistance

In December 1989, Myanmar and China signed an instrument of economic and technical cooperation agreement. In 1991, China gave a grant of Yuan 50 million and in 1993; Myanmar received an interest-free loan of Yuan 50 million from China.

In 2003, during the visit of General Than Shwe to China, the Chinese government gave a grant of yet another 50 million Yuan and a loan of USD 200 million as preferential credit. The grant was for construction of a combine harvester plant in Ingone and three small-scale hydroelectric projects. Due to the sheer secrecy in China and Myanmar, reliable data was not available for a long time and the fact that there is no distinction between China's state-owned enterprises and state-commercial investments makes it difficult to obtain numerical evidence of China's complete investment and economic support to Myanmar.

Infrastructure Creation

Due to lack of funds at the disposal of the then Myanmar government, Chinese infrastructure development is another important aspect of economic assistance in the decades of the 1900s and 2000. Chinese companies were busy building roads, dams and ports, using low-interest loans and export credit. For example, China was building the less-known Tasang Dam on the Salween river, which will be integrated into the Greater Mekong sub-region power grid. Since 1988, China has helped the Myanmar government in many ways. It has built eight or nine sugar mills (worth USD 158 million), 20 hydroelectric projects (worth USD 269 million) and many new factories for the Ministry of Industry. China also upgraded six existing factories for the Ministry (worth USD 346 million). It provided six ocean vessels and built a dry dockyard (worth USD 25 million). In 2006, Chinese firms built seven new hydro-electric plants (worth USD 350-400 million).

In a nutshell, foreign investment and technological transfers from China to Myanmar were clearly aimed to increase the value of exports. It is well known that China's development assistance is closely associated to Chinese business interests in Myanmar. Commercial loans were provided with a clear aim so that Chinese firms could benefit from China's development programme. This helps China to secure the supply of semi-finished goods for its growing economy. In addition, it squarely secures China's geopolitical interests in the entire Indian Ocean region.

Arms and Technological Assistance

Ever since the military takeover of power in Myanmar in 1988, it is believed that through barter deals and interest-free loans, China has equipped Myanmar's army with military hardware including tanks, armoured personnel carriers, military aircraft and artillery weapons such as howitzers, anti-tank guns and anti-aircraft guns. Also, post-1998, the United Nations reported that China has delivered USD 5.9 million worth of military hardware to Myanmar under the category of 'tanks and other armoured fighting vehicles,' and USD 3.4 million of 'military weapons.' In addition, the PLA also provided training in the technical use of the weapons systems.

Political Umbrella

China used its permanent membership in the UN Security Council to provide a political anchor to Myanmar's military *Junta* regime till 2010. In 2007, the UN prepared a resolution that holistically condemned Myanmar's human rights violations which was vetoed by China. Had that resolution been passed, it would have enabled international human rights organizations to operate without restriction and begin a political dialogue with all stakeholders in that country.

As it is well known, China sees itself as a future superpower and to achieve its goal, it needs to augment its regional and international influence manifold. Myanmar provided a rare opportunity to China to ensure access to its vast natural resources and to some extent improved China's international image of assisting Myanmar in crisis. China wants to continue to explore Myanmar's natural resources and have friendly relations with the government in power to guarantee border stability and protect its investments which will result in high returns. Besides, the strategic position of Myanmar compelled China to maintain its relations with the then military *Junta* to become less dependent on the Malacca Strait and secure its oil transportation across the Indian Ocean.

Obstacles to China's Interests in Myanmar

In recent years, there has been a conscious attempt by China to balance its economic development with its international reputation. Four factors will trouble China from reaching its goal:

(a) Increase in border instability.
(b) Growing resentment against the Chinese.
(c) Weak Myanmar governance.
(d) Growing international pressure on China to be more involved in Myanmar.

Border Instability: The economic growth of any country has a direct relation with its internal stability. China has made it a priority to maintain border stability in order to pursue its economic development. In 2009, when Myanmar conducted military operations against the Kokang, Myanmar National Democratic Alliance Army (MNDAA), more than 50,000 people ran into Chinese territory. China responded immediately by providing food, shelter and medical attention.

In addition, China then immediately deployed extra troops and armed policemen at the border to prevent a possible spillover of the violence into its territory and prevented China-Myanmar ties from snapping. The Kokang are of Chinese ancestry; they speak Mandarin and have lived for decades in the hills of Northeast Myanmar. This military operation led to a slight diplomatic scuffle between the two countries. China was "deeply upset" with the Myanmar government for not informing it of the military operation. Subsequently, Myanmar had to apologize to the Chinese for the instability caused by its offensive. With this example, it can be seen that China holds border stability as a key factor to the peaceful development of China and therefore it is working hard to curb all kinds of illegal activities such as narcotics trade, prostitution, HIV/AIDS and gambling along its border.

Drugs and Gambling

The Golden Triangle, which includes Myanmar, had been the epicentre of the opium and heroin trade in the 1980s and even today 95 per cent of the heroin in China comes from this region. The Chinese authorities believe that there is a sure correlation between drugs and crime as well as drugs and sex, which can lead to the spread of HIV/AIDS. In addition, since gambling is forbidden in China, many Chinese nationals have gone to bordering countries to play in casinos. From the Chinese government's perspective, gambling can lead to kidnappings, torture and murders of people unable to repay debts. Therefore, China has taken strong action against these illegal activities.

Growing Resentment against China

In spite of China's huge economic investments in Myanmar for the last 25 years, it has not led to a visible social development due to China's lack of trust on Myanmar and the latter's lack of investment in its own society. This has made the locals resent Chinese presence and Chinese projects in Myanmar. There is an unequal economic investment between the two nations. Taking the period from the 1990s to 2006, Myanmar's imports from China grew at a much faster pace than its exports to China. In 1990, Myanmar's exports to China were a meagre USD 33 million and in 2006 they had increased 6.9 times, reaching USD 229.7 million. During the same period, its imports were USD 137.7 million and exports increased 9.6 times to USD 1.098 billion.

Many problems have arisen over a period of time from this unequal trade: firstly, there has been growing dissatisfaction with the quality of Chinese goods; secondly, a feeling of neo-colonialism and suppression has developed and; thirdly, the depletion of natural resources without enough compensation to the locals.

Chinese Products

Since the 1970s Chinese goods have flooded the Myanmar markets mostly through illegal trade. Just like the rest of the world, every household in Myanmar purchases cheap Chinese products. However, there has been a growing resentment against the quality of these goods. Moreover, once these products arrive in the cities in Myanmar's interior, they become more expensive due to middlemen along the way.

Feeling of Alienation

In the northern part where Mandarin is spoken widely, there is an increase of signs translated into Chinese. A lot of businesses have some kind of Chinese investment and some have estimated that China owns 60 per cent of Myanmar's economy in Central Mandalay state, which was being unofficially renamed as 'Chinatown.'

Environmental Degradation

There is little and mostly unreliable information on land acquisition, environmental impact and displacement by Chinese hydropower, mining, wood trade, oil and gas exploration projects, which have raised concerns of international organizations as well as local bodies, especially after 2010 when the press sanctions were lifted in Myanmar. Chinese construction and infrastructure development projects do not involve the locals due to the lack of confidence on Myanmar's labour force; the Chinese instead bring thousands of their own labourers for their projects in Myanmar. Hence, there is little economic input in the local economy. In addition, these infrastructure projects have to be protected due to instability and necessitate a large labour force thereby promoting military presence, forced labour and forced relocation.

Weak Governance in Myanmar

Efficient economic trade between any two countries demands a stable socio-political environment. Thus, it was in China's own interest that Myanmar should have strong governance. Confidence in a country to secure, provide and achieve economic trade is based on the political atmosphere. A weak Myanmarese government which was under UN sanctions always threatened Chinese investments. Myanmar's lack of expertise and knowledge of trade and economic policies made China's investments insecure.

In 2007, China tried to establish Special Economic Zones (SEZ), just like it had done on its territory in the early 1990s but Myanmar's inability to understand the SEZ concept and lack of economic expertise resulted in its failure to pass a law that would have helped develop the country. The then Myanmar government, which is known to be mired in corruption, a weak judicial system and total lack of transparency and accountability made it difficult to do business in Myanmar. Even Chinese businessmen complained of widespread corruption. Myanmar's inability to provide a safe and secure environment for trade, combined with a lack of professionalism and widespread corruption, made it appear that China's investments stand on loose sand. Therefore, it is in China's interest to ensure the stability of Myanmar's socio-politico environment that includes building relations with ethnic groups and the military regime. As most of the natural resources are located in territories inhabited by ethnic minorities, China is trying to maintain strong relations with ethnic groups. According to the International Crisis Group (ICG), China wants to maintain a balance of power between ethnic groups and the government to ensure the maintenance of stability under which China can exploit the resources of the country. China too has its fair share of ethnic minorities and knows well the importance of preventing ethnic groups from gaining full autonomy. China is afraid that such autonomy could lead to instability in the border areas since nearly 25 of the 55 ethnic minorities live in Yunnan province.

It is a known fact that China helps and supports these minorities especially the Kachin, Wa and Kokang by providing economic as well as arms and basic utilities assistance. Myanmar's government does not approve these relations because they undermine its authority as the government which continues to fight these groups. At times, China can leverage its relations with the ethnic minorities while dealing with the Myanmar government. Consequently, Myanmar's government did not fully trust China and tried to limit Chinese influence in its internal and external policies, especially after 2010, when quasi-military government came to power with Aung San Suu Kyi becoming the leader of the opposition in the House.

Earlier, China had invested and financed many projects in Myanmar. It did not expect an immediate return but believed that in the long term it would be beneficial for China's economic development. Therefore, it is essential for China to maintain good relations with ethnic groups that live in resource-rich areas and with Myanmar's government to gain official access to these resources. This 'two-faced' policy which China applied in the past and is employing even now, albeit in a subtle manner, can be very dangerous and unstable but guarantees China's access to Myanmar's resources. Just like the British 'divide and rule' policy, China wants to maintain this relationship for economic purposes to prevent internal instability vis-à-vis its own ethnic minorities and gain some leverage over Myanmar's government for business and trade.

CHINA'S RISE TO SUPERPOWER STATUS

The Limits of Human Rights Violations

China's unique political system and history makes it extra tolerant of human rights violations but there is a limit to Chinese support for governments having cases of human rights violations. Although it is impossible to define such limits, China's support was clearly visible in spite of Myanmar's blatant human rights violations from 1990 to 2010. Great international pressure on China was affecting its reputation. Hence, China, in recent years, has tried to balance economic trade interests and its international image by becoming more involved in international humanitarian aid during the 2008 Cyclone Nargis.

The 2007 Saffron Revolution

During the 2007 Saffron revolution in Myanmar, China faced strong international pressure to take a stronger stand against the military regime and so China supported the Security Council statement and resolution on violence against peaceful protestors. China immediately called for democratic process and political dialogue with the opposition. It is believed that China's influence during the crisis was deeply affected by its decision to join the international community against the military regime. China faced criticism from Myanmar for "siding with them." Despite Myanmar's condemnation, China is still providing strong diplomatic support to the UN. It even supported the UN Security Council statement of 2008 that expressed disappointment at Myanmar's slow progress on the Seven Step Roadmap to Democracy which led Myanmar to establish a timeline for the same.

The Saffron Revolution was an eye-opening experience for the international community; they witnessed a pro-active China that had the will to improve the human rights situation that had been prevailing for a long time in Myanmar. Although China made sure that the UN Resolution was softer than the original draft, it was one of those rare times that China did not defend its economic partner.

2008 Cyclone Nargis in Myanmar

In 2008, Myanmar was struck with a very serious natural disaster in which hundreds of people lost their lives and faced high scale devastation. Myanmar's military regime refused to accept international aid. China played an important role in convincing the military generals to accept aid.

In November 2008, about 14 pro-democratic activists in Myanmar were given 65 years of prison sentences due to their involvement in the 2007 Revolution. The Chinese Foreign Minister advised Myanmar's regime to reduce the sentence to 3-4 years to diminish international attention. According to a diplomat, "the Chinese are actively trying to ensure that the regime does not go too far. Neither does China does want a US-oriented state on its border, nor does it want a pariah state on its border."

Aung San Suu Kyi and China

After the decision to extend Aung San Suu Kyi's prison term by 18 months, a Chinese official said that the world should respect the judicial sovereignty of Myanmar. In addition, China said that it would oppose any UN statement against the verdict and as a result the UN press statement just expressed "serious concern" regarding the situation.

During the Ninth Asia-Foreign Ministers meeting, China expressed its discontent and serious concern about the Aung San Suu Kyi situation. The ministers agreed for the release of all those in detention and for lifting of restrictions on political parties. In addition, China joined the Group of Friends in calling for the release of Aung San Suu Kyi and other political prisoners in Myanmar. So, in other words, China kept playing the double card.

Economic Growth vs Political Ambition

There is a clear dilemma between China's economic growth and its international reputation. The timing of these events is important; the Olympics was a great opportunity to project itself as 'Grand China,' one that has a great history, culture and economy and is the future world power. China's joining the international community in its stand against Myanmar was not driven by altruistic motives but clearly because China was gaining either through economic growth or the improvement of its international reputation.

China is certainly cautious about its position on Myanmar-related issues as it has very large investments and is expecting high returns. Greater international sanctions on Myanmar would affect China's international image which would put pressure on its economic ties with Myanmar. On the one hand, it has business deals, and on the other, the political ambition to become a superpower, thereby, demanding some economic sacrifice on its part. China wants to become a regional and international superpower which will entail the responsibility of promoting higher and better standards for human rights, economic growth and global peace. Therefore, China has demonstrated in recent years a more active position in the international arena but still abstained from taking an overt critical stance against the Myanmar military regime till 2010.

What Did Myanmar Seek from China?

Myanmar understands that it is strategically located between the two regional giants—China and India—both of which have the ambition to become world powers. In addition, Myanmar's natural wealth and China's thirst for the same have made these resources economically valuable, thus, bringing greater income to the existing military regime. In exchange for assuring regional trade, Myanmar was confident that China will completely support the military government and even trade which is important for the country's economic and political sustainability.

It is a well-known fact that China is the largest investor in Myanmar, but Myanmar is far from being 'controlled' by the dragon. It can also be argued that it is China that is being manipulated by Myanmar and not vice versa. As discussed in the previous section, China provides a wide range of services from financial support to infrastructure building in Myanmar, but Myanmar still keeps the upper hand in this unequal relationship. Myanmar uses China for its economic needs, political support in the international community and, most importantly, while negotiating with other regional or international players for resource exploitation. From 1990 to 2010, Myanmar's military regime played upon its key strategic geographic location and abundance of natural resources with China, India and

ASEAN countries. Myanmar is surrounded by developing countries; and energy requirement is the foundation for any country to grow and prosper.

In this context, where Myanmar has the 'resources' a large number of countries have the 'requirement,' so the astute regime used its strategic leverage to gain economic growth to sustain its political system. Myanmar also used its close relations with China to influence and increase its leverage with other powers such as India and ASEAN to achieve its goals of economic and political support for the development of the military to legitimize its hold on power.

Myanmar Regime Played with China and India

It is important to mention that political legitimacy generally is defined in terms of economic trade; when countries agree to trade with another government, whether they overtly or covertly support the government does not matter, their business ties legitimize the government in place. In this sense, Myanmar is a legitimate government because of its strong regional and international trade relations with China and India (after it introduced its LOOK EAST POLICY in 1996). I will show how Myanmar gained political legitimacy through economic and political recognition with China and India. Myanmar understands the competition between China and India. By maximizing on this situation, Myanmar maintains the upper hand; hypothetically, if India is not ready to pay for goods at the price desired, China or ASEAN will do it, and vice versa. So creating such competition provided more economic support to the regime and therefore it provides political legitimacy.

The recent bidding war between China and India for the Shwe project demonstrated Myanmar's regional importance for the growth of both countries. From the Indian perspective, Myanmar is the door to South Asia and Southeast Asia. From the Chinese perspective, Myanmar presents a big untapped market and additional routes for natural resources. China and India are both only looking at access to existing raw material and energy resources in Myanmar. For Shwe oil and gas, China won the bid to be the sole operator (50.1%) with

Myanmar Oil and Gas Enterprise (MOGE) holding 49.1 per cent to distribute the oil through its two pipelines (oil and gas). The estimated cost of construction of both pipelines combined was USD 3.5 billion in addition to the development of off-shore fields for gas components worth USD 3 billion. In addition, the China National Petroleum Corporation (CNPC) is presently paying an annual transit fee of USD 150 million per year to the regime for use of the pipeline in Myanmar. The oil and gas pipelines commenced operations in 2013.

China has commissioned two pipelines: one for oil from the Middle East and Africa to be offloaded from tankers at a Myanmar port and then piped into Yunnan province of China. This 793-km pipeline starts from Kuaykphyu in Myanmar and passes through Rakhine state, Magway and Mandalay regions into Shan State and then enters China at Ruili in Yunnan province. Enroute the pipeline has six pumping stations. The cost of this gas pipeline has been estimated at USD 2.01 billion. The gas pipeline has a pumping capacity of 12 billion cubic metres and that of the oil pipeline is 22 million tonnes of crude oil per year. Just by allowing the transit, Myanmar is going to have multifarious benefits. The annual transmission of 22 million tons of crude oil through the pipeline will bring $ 22 million as well as $ 13.6 million in transit fees. Exporting 12 billion cubic metres of gas will bring in $ 1.5 billion. This means a lot to the weak and struggling economy of the nation. Myanmar also gets rights to use 2 billion cubic metres of natural gas for its domestic use. This is likely to be used by major cities along the pipeline to supply energy to the inland regions thus boosting its economy. Over the next 30 years, Myanmar is set to earn a whopping $ 30 billion from this project. As per an independent local news network in Myanmar, www.mizzima.com, this project will create a huge amount of job opportunities for local people by the hiring of as many as over 6,000 persons for the construction work followed by maintenance work.

On the one hand, China wants political stability in the country because of its economic investment. On the other, it gains political legitimacy by acting as the mediator between Myanmar and the international community. It is a win-win situation for Myanmar and

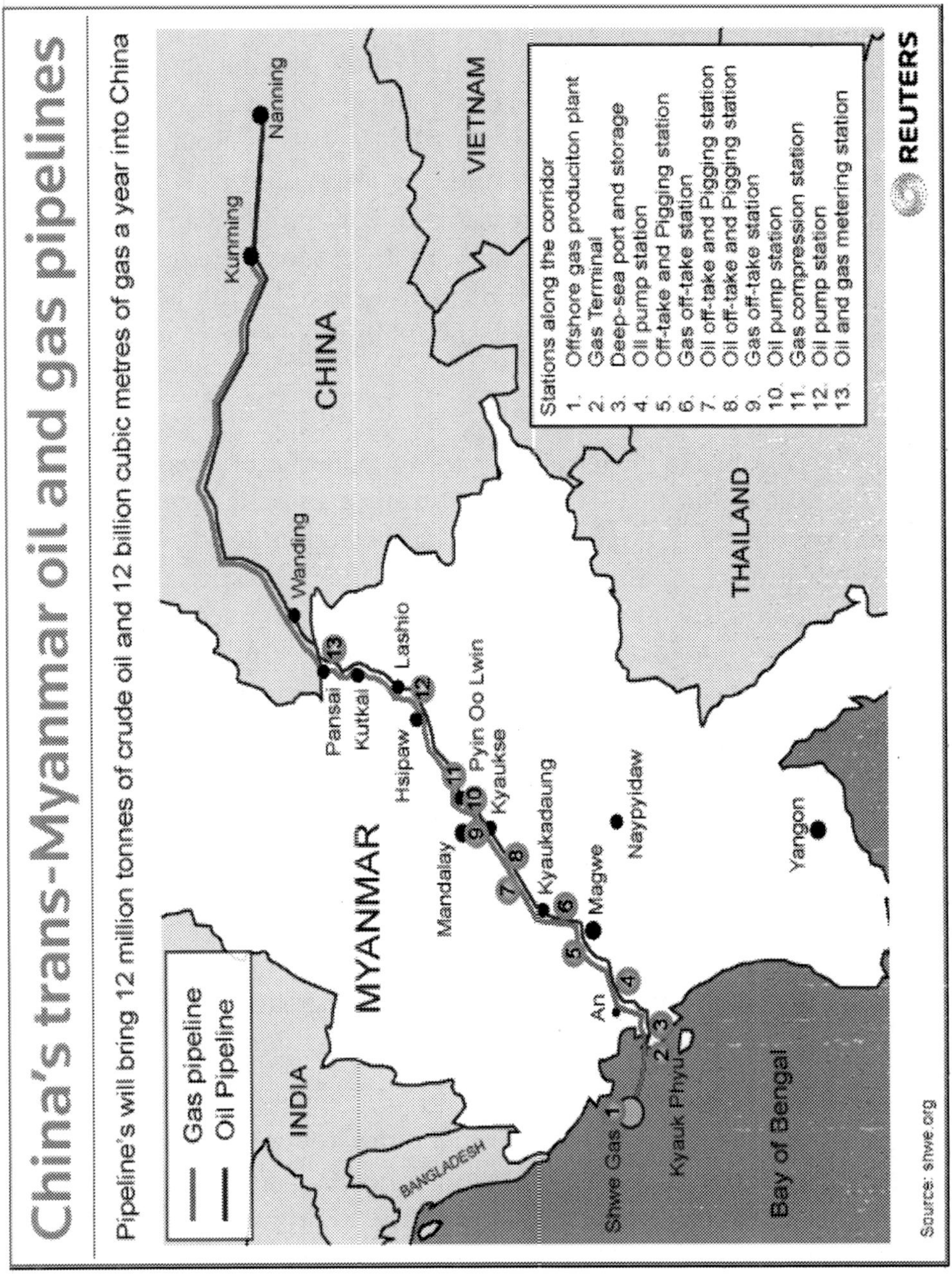
China's trans-Myanmar oil and gas pipelines
Pipeline's will bring 12 million tonnes of crude oil and 12 billion cubic metres of gas a year into China
Gas pipeline
Oil Pipeline
INDIA
BANGLADESH
MYANMAR
CHINA
VIETNAM
THAILAND
Bay of Bengal
Shwe Gas
Kyauk Phyu
An
Magwe
Kyaukadaung
Mandalay
Kyaukse
Pyin Oo Lwin
Hsipaw
Lashio
Kutkai
Pansai
Wanding
Kunming
Nanning
Naypyidaw
Yangon
Stations along the corridor
1. Offshore gas produciton plant
2. Gas Terminal
3. Deep-sea port and storage
4. Oil pump station
5. Off-take and Pigging station
6. Gas off-take station
7. Oil off-take and Pigging station
8. Oil off-take and Pigging station
9. Gas off-take station
10. Oil pump station
11. Gas compression station
12. Oil pump station
13. Oil and gas metering station
Source: shwe.org
REUTERS

China since both gain either strategic access or political credibility. As China provided and is still providing financial support to the regime, it helps to sustain its power as a result which it allows China to have some level of preferential treatment regarding the exploitation of natural resources. Over the last two decades, China has been providing advice and support and has also acted as a mediator between Myanmar and the international community. China's large economy provides the country with political and strategic leverage and Myanmar's military government used it to its full advantage. The stand of the new government under Htin Kyaw is yet to be seen.

Trade and Energy Relations

China has established itself as a key trading partner of Myanmar and there is little doubt that China has a strong economic leverage over Myanmar, but this influence at times has been double-edged. Over a period of time, China has increased its influence, especially in the northern border region of Myanmar. Yunnan, a province of China, is one of China's poorest regions and has the lowest productivity rates. From this angle, Myanmar is a golden opportunity for Chinese companies based in Yunnan. The abundance of natural resources in Myanmar makes the country highly attractive for investment. However, the mentality demonstrated by some Chinese companies in Myanmar has had a severe negative impact on the environment through unsustainable usage, ethically wrong policies and outperforming local Myanmar businesses. It is also negative for the overall perception of the Chinese at large. China's reputation has plummeted greatly because of this. There is a great deal of criticism of China to be heard both among the minorities as well as the government and political opponents.

It is clear that China sees Myanmar more from a strategic point of view than the regional government in Yunnan does which is looking beyond solely business interests that often tend to be focused on short-term gains. It has created notable resentment against China in general and the Chinese in particular. Investments and trade have flourished between China and Myanmar in huge volumes mainly due to international boycotts which have forced Myanmar to work with anyone willing and on any terms. According to Myanmar's official statistics, China is increasingly dominating Myanmar's economy. This might be the reason for the sensitivity in Myanmar over China's economic influence. Concurrent with this development, India has become a significant export market for Myanmar and is now at par with China's official trade with Myanmar. In fact, the illegal markets are major avenues of economic interaction. The trade in narcotics that has had a devastating effect on Yunnan's capital, Kunming, which is often referred to as 'the drug capital of China.' The amount of this trade is difficult to estimate, but over a period of time trade in opium and heroin has decreased with the opening of Afghani markets. Trade in natural resources, humans, and methamphetamine has also increased to a great extent.

Table 1: Myanmar's Top 5 Export and Import Partners (2016)

Import	*Trade (US$ Mil)*	*Partner share(%)*
China	4,767	40.84
Thailand	2,241	19.20
India	1,038	8.89
Singapore	891	7.63
Japan	663	5.68

Exporter	*Trade (US$ Mil)*	*Partner share(%)*
China	5,403	34.42
Singapore	2,268	14.45
Thailand	1,986	12.65
Japan	1,255	7.99
India	1,095	6.97

Source: World Bank. https://wits.worldbank.org/CountryProfile/en/Country/MMR/Year/LTST/Summary

It can be seen from Table 1 that there is a strong increase in Chinese investments and trade with Myanmar, yet available statistics are useful only for indicating trends. However, there is a formal market that is significantly undervalued as well as large grey and black markets whose size remains largely unfathomed. This is especially true in strategic areas such as natural resources and even the weapons industry. China has begun to initiate a number of large infrastructure projects in Myanmar and their magnitude, both in size and economy, will grow as the oil and gas pipelines and the added surface transport system through Myanmar increases. With the increasing infrastructure investments, China's FDI in Myanmar will quickly outpace the FDI of all the others. It has been noted that China has already engaged in 17 large oil and gas projects in Myanmar during 2009. It is a trade in all regions of the world that has grown increasingly important for China but which, for geographical reasons, is particularly beneficial to Myanmar. One should not see Myanmar's importance as limited only to the economic arena or its role as a provider of natural resources. The country has also developed into a strategically very important transport and shipping hub. Myanmar ports could easily be useful as a shortcut to China's inland areas in the south, providing a friendly harbour in times of need. Harbours on Myanmar coastline should be considered as part of a larger network of transport corridors which includes Gwadar. China is extremely interested in diversifying its current transport routes as 80 per cent of its imported oil passes through the Malacca Strait which is known to be controlled by the USA and the strait would be easy to close, either intentionally, by mistake, or simply due to some natural disaster. There is a view among the leaders in Beijing that China's over-dependence on the Malacca Strait can be used against China.

China-Myanmar Strategic Relations

China-Myanmar strategic ties are a recent phenomenon. However, the strategic importance of Myanmar for China has undergone serious fluctuations since the country's formation. In 1949, after establishment of the People's Republic of China (PRC) Myanmar (then Burma) was the first non-socialist country to establish diplomatic ties with the PRC and a friend that helped China to break its international isolation. Till 2000, political friendship was the only highlight of bilateral relations that had fluctuated to a great extent owing to the interference of the Communist Party of China. Around 1990, as Myanmar was isolated by the rest of the world it had little choice but to approach China, who along with helping began to seek new resources and markets; the economic cooperation between the two countries picked up speed. Myanmar is located along the Chinese border and rich in natural resources (such as hydropower, minerals, timber, and jade), turned out to be an easy destination for Chinese investment. Beginning with border trade, the economic campaign soon became dominated by large Chinese state-owned enterprises seeking energy and mineral supplies from Myanmar. By 2010, China became Myanmar's biggest investor and second largest trading partner. During this period Myanmar, as a supplier of natural resources and raw materials, achieved a highly important status as an economic partner of China. Thus, political friendship and economic cooperation were the two pivots of China's relationship with Myanmar, with little or no specific mention of the country's strategic importance. Analysts had begun talking about Myanmar as a corridor into the Indian Ocean for China but there was no strategic partnership treaty between the two. China, in general, did not actively seek to build a formal or strong strategic relationship with Myanmar. With China's national interests and increasing influence in the region, Myanmar's strategic importance for it increased. This importance is manifested through four initiatives taken by China with the Thein Sein government: the establishment of a comprehensive strategic partnership; China's seeking of Myanmar's support in regional diplomacy; the potential enhancement of military cooperation; and Yunnan's bridgehead strategy.

Generally, China's strategic interests can be divided into:

1. Maintaining access to the Indian Ocean to counter Indian presence;
2. Countering any attempt to encircle China;
3. Stabilizing the Chinese border with Myanmar; and
4. Preventing the spillover of Myanmar-ethnic conflicts into China.

It is well known that China has a strong influence in the regions of Myanmar bordering China. This is primarily due to the problems created by Myanmar ethnic groups of Chinese origin and Chinese immigrants living in border areas. China has clearly shown interest in using Myanmar as a future springboard to the Indian Ocean. Based on China's fear of containment and the increasing costs of trade there are some limitations that China encounters while dealing with Myanmar. Naypyidaw is seriously concerned over China's influence in Myanmar.

Myanmar, for its part, always had an interest in utilizing Chinese assistance in

1. breaking the international boycott.
2. reducing the tensions with the minority groups in the northern part of the country, including some of Chinese descent.
3. Managing Chinese interests and immigrants.

Myanmar understands that although its interests are more often than not in conflict with China, it is crucial that it avoids challenging its giant neighbour. Despite this, the relations are often described as warm and cordial. The government of Myanmar has very little latitude with China and is in a relationship which can best be described as 'dependent.' In 2009 the Kokang incident , when the Myanmar army cracked down on weapons production in the northern border area, resulted in a refugee flow of 30,000 people into China. This incident was significant as it showed that the Chinese were not happy with the handling of the situation and Myanmar's foreign ministry later apologized. Over the last few decades, China has been saying that it will not engage in Myanmar's internal affairs. But the direct involvement of Chinese business houses engaging local and regional companies in Myanmar has been viewed by Naypyidaw as involvement in Myanmar's internal affairs.

This has not only been criticized in the Myanmar government but also at regional and local levels. The Chinese government has been somewhat critical of how different groups in China have behaved but it has not acted in any clear manner against them. The illegal border trade in narcotics has become a big security threat to China and poses serious problems. However, with effective border control by the Chinese and competition from Afghanistan, the threat has reduced considerably. There is a 'string of pearls' in terms of port facilities that China has constructed or is constructing ranging from Sihanoukville (Cambodia), Laem Chabang (Thailand), Kyaukphyu (Myanmar), Chittagong (Bangladesh), Hambantota (Sri Lanka) to Gwadar (Pakistan). Such a network of port facilities managed by governments that are friendly towards China will improve its security situation both economically and militarily.

The military component appears less important in the medium term. Port facilities in Myanmar have an important position within such a network and are important in securing China's economic interests between the oil-rich Gulf and China. Due to its geographical location, China has greater use of the port facilities in Myanmar, as goods can be taken north directly into China if needed and any strategic base in Myanmar could be reinforced by the land route, if Myanmar permits it at a later stage. As of now there are only two pipelines, one for gas the other for crude oil. Before a major port facility is constructed, China needs to first make sure that it has the capacity to protect and utilize its own facilities and perhaps more importantly needs to develop its strategic naval interests beyond Myanmar.

China has connections with a number of ports in Myanmar, such as Hainggyi, Coco Island, Sittwe, Zadetkyi, Myeik and Kyaukphyu. To assume that these ports are a sign of Chinese military expansion and potential aggression against India or other states in the region is problematic. At the same time, there seems to be no doubt that China has an interest in developing port facilities for both military and civilian purposes—but there is little evidence that this strategy has been successful.

This has given rise to a great deal of scepticism over the purposes for disseminating this information. It is clear that China's long-term intention is to cultivate closer naval and military cooperation with a number of Southeast Asian states. The development of a strong Chinese maritime presence can be related to modernization of the Chinese military, in which the navy or PLAN as it is generally referred to, is relatively weak in terms of blue water capacity and force projection. This had resulted in a modest Chinese interest in naval bases in Southeast Asia. By 2050, China is expected to achieve world-class blue water navy status. Myanmar would be strategically important for China to achieve direct access to the Pacific and the Indian oceans. The PLAN would be able to shorten the distance by 3000 kilometres reducing the voyage by five to six days by not passing through the Strait of Malacca to reach the Bay of Bengal. In 1994, Japanese sources reported that China had completed construction of radar and electronic surveillance facilities on the Coco Islands which were on lease to China. It should also be noted that the scepticism from the military regime in the late 1990s in Naypyidaw over relying too much on China had led Myanmar to open its ports of Sittwe and Dawei for use by the Indian Navy. This fits the Indian strategy of creating a fleet of 130 vessels comprising three aircraft battle groups by 2020 to counter Chinese influence. Similarly, many senior leaders in the Myanmar armed forces and also, especially after the 2010 elections, the government under Mr Thein Sein, had seriously raised the possibility of increased cooperation with the USA and Europe in a big way after they had begun to lift the sanctions.

Comprehensive Strategic Cooperative Partnership

In May 2011, when the then President of Myanmar, Mr Thein Sein, visited Beijing, China and Myanmar signed the 'Comprehensive Strategic Cooperative Partnership.' Thus, the long bilateral ties between China and Myanmar were elevated to a strategic partnership thus signalling a new definition of the affiliation. The specifics of what this partnership will constitute was emphasised by Chinese President Hu Jintao. He mentioned four basic components: elevating bilateral relations and expanding exchanges and cooperation at all levels, strengthening mutual strategic support, deepening pragmatic cooperation and maintaining border stability. The first and the last components revisit old territory, as China has always aspired to improve relations and maintain border stability. The other two, however, indicated certain new elements in China's aspirations in Myanmar. Firstly, 'mutual strategic support' signals China's expectation for reciprocity from Myanmar on strategic issues. In other words, Beijing hopes for higher coordination with Myanmar to support its position on regional multilateral platforms like ASEAN, turning Myanmar into a useful ally to support the Chinese regional foreign policy agenda. Secondly, 'mutually beneficial and pragmatic cooperation' meant that China's economic relationship with Myanmar has to benefit both countries. President Hu pointed out several areas for increased cooperation in which China was interested, which included energy, power, agriculture and transport. He also emphasized the importance of the completion of large projects currently under construction. Thirdly, according to him, the establishment of the comprehensive strategic cooperative partnership was the key component of the partnership concerns regarding Myanmar's role in regional multilateral platforms. China wishes to "coordinate with Myanmar on ASEAN+3, ASEAN+1, and the Greater Mekong Sub-Regional Economic Cooperation to protect the interests of Myanmar and China."

Military Cooperation between China and Myanmar

One of the most discussed issues is the growing military cooperation between Myanmar and China. There is little doubt that China has emerged as the most important provider to Myanmar of military equipment and training since 1988 after the military regime took over power and after the 1990s when it refused to transfer power to the democratically elected government after the elections. Most of the countries had imposed trade sanctions against the military regime as it indulged in large-scale human rights abuse. At that time, China came to its rescue in the international arena; hence, the earlier not-so-cordial ties saw a change and since the 1988 post-military coup period, Myanmar has cemented closer civil, trade and military cooperation with China. In 1989, the first military delegation arrived in Beijing to negotiate the purchase of arms from China. A deal worth about USD 1.4 billion was struck. Besides the supply of arms, (jet fighters, tanks, naval ships, etc.) China also agreed to train Myanmar's air force, military and army personnel. The aim of these hasty arms purchases was to enhance Myanmar's military might and use them to suppress the ebullient ethnic insurgencies. In 1994, Myanmar received another stock of USD 400 million worth of arms.

In 1996, the visit of Myanmar Army Chief, General Maung Aye, to China resulted in further enhancement of military and intelligence cooperation between the two neighbours. China agreed to even train 300 personnel from the Myanmar air force and some naval officers and to provide additional places for them in the Chinese Staff College. Thereafter, China also offered favourable terms for Myanmar's arms purchases by offering free loans and giving some on credit, as well as economic aid and investments for the construction of Myanmar's basic infrastructure like dams, bridges, roads, ports and numerous industrial projects. Construction of roads along the Irrawaddy River to link Yunnan province with the Bay of Bengal were of significant strategic importance.

However, over the past decade, Myanmar's military forces have diversified their imports due to the inferior quality of some Chinese weapons systems (as the Chinese did not sell their best equipment) to reduce Myanmar's dependence on a single importer and to get better quality arms. For Myanmar, Russia, India, Pakistan and possibly North Korea have also emerged as additional suppliers of weapons. This shift in import preferences is particularly prevalent in more advanced weapons systems, which the Myanmar military is increasingly trying to buy from some country other than China. Russia, to take one example, sold twenty MiG-29s to Myanmar for USD 570 million. China has never been the most sought-after provider of military equipment for Myanmar, but has come to play that role out of necessity rather than choice for Myanmar. Due to the heavy investments already committed, this is not likely to change in the short-term despite improved relations with the EU and the USA, but could over a period of time result in a diversification of trade thereby decreasing Myanmar's reliance on China and other traditional providers of military equipment. In 2011, before the establishment of the comprehensive strategic cooperative partnership, China sent the most senior military delegation headed by the No. 4 leader of China's supreme military command, Central Military Commission (CMC) Vice Chairman Xu Caihou to coordinate the nuances of military cooperation.

After the restoration of democracy in 2016, there is the likelihood of new players seeing Myanmar as a potential market. There has been a notable effort from Beijing to ensure that its special relationship with Myanmar will not negatively impact China's relationship with other Southeast Asian countries or its long-term position in the region. There have been consistent attempts from China to clarify this through official and unofficial channels. This policy is not pursued because of Chinese good-heartedness but is at least partly due to the risk that such sales would entail for its own border security as well as the impact it might have on other countries in the region.

Yunnan's Bridgehead Strategy

In 2011, China launched its Twelfth Five Year Plan in which it formally announced the national 'bridgehead strategy' which proposed to turn Yunnan into a strategic corridor and a bridgehead for China's strategic engagement in the Indian Ocean. China's only coastal line is on the eastern side, leading to the strategic prioritization of the Pacific Ocean. For central and eastern China, it is more convenient to use the Indian Ocean as an outlet. The bridgehead strategy will free China from the 'strategic passiveness' of the 'One Ocean Strategy.' The bridgehead strategy itself is candid proof of China's pursuit of the 'Two Ocean Strategy' and depicts China's strategic assertiveness in the Indian Ocean.

A more cogent reason, as per some thinkers, is that China wants a more active Indian Ocean strategy and for this it is turning Pakistan and Myanmar into outposts of China's strategic outreach into the Indian Ocean.

Setbacks to China's Myanmar Strategy

In spite of having made very concrete plans to include Myanmar in its overall strategic plan, China has encountered numerous obstacles and setbacks since 2011. President Thein Sein's decision to suspend the $ 3.4 billion Myitsone dam project on September 30, 2011 because of a public outcry over environmental issues was a major setback and was followed by rapid improvement of relations with the USA and the visit by President Obama. Myanmar's quick moves surprised and frustrated China, forcing it to re-align its strategies towards Myanmar.

Myitsone Dam Suspension

In 2011, when Myanmar government suspended the Myitsone Dam project, the decision came as a surprise to China. Although, from the beginning, the project had been controversial and had faced tremendous public opposition, China analysts never thought that Naypyidaw would dare to jeopardise a project of such large scale and great importance. This confidence was based on the belief that an isolated Naypyidaw would not risk antagonizing its largest political and economic mentor over a dam project. China attributes the suspension decision to both internal and external factors in Myanmar. On the one hand, China feels the dam project is the victim of Myanmar's urge to improve relations with the USA and on the other hand China realized that there is a strong anti-China sentiment in Myanmar. In the meantime, China hoped that differences on this project could be resolved through subtle negotiations. Some analysts suggested that the plan could be revised as a complete abandonment would be 'humiliating' for China.

Furthermore, China Power International had already invested more than $ 42 million in the Myitsone dam. Its suspension has a major impact on China's perception of and relationship with Myanmar. Most analysts believe that this project suspension 'fundamentally' shook Chinese leaders' trust in Myanmar as a strategic partner and is certainly going to have a long-term impact over how they perceive Myanmar's reliability and trustworthiness.

U.S.–Myanmar Engagement

China's strategic engagement plan for Myanmar was based on the assumption that the domestic politics of Myanmar would not undergo much changes in the near future, keeping in view that the country is isolated internationally and subject to serious economic sanctions by the West. Myanmar did not have any other source to fulfil its needs. However, the rapid improvement of relations between the USA and Myanmar after 2010 proved China totally wrong, causing China to lose its monopolistic edge in Myanmar. Although the Obama Administration had announced its Myanmar strategy as early as in 2009, China thought this would never materialise while there is military government in Myanmar. The condemnation of the 2010 elections by the White House as "neither open nor democratic" reassured China that a rapid improvement of bilateral relations was highly unlikely. However, in 2011, after President Thein Sein's meeting with Aung San Suu Kyi, U.S.–Myanmar relations began to improve. Not only did U.S. Special Envoy Derek Mitchell pay a number of visits but Secretary of State Hillary Clinton also travelled to Myanmar three months later. It was followed by Clinton's announcement that the USA would be sending its ambassadors to Myanmar in January 2012. Subsequently, Mr Thein Sein also travelled to the USA and President Obama made a short visit to Myanmar which changed the tide in the relations.

Beijing's fear of this rapid improvement of U.S.–Myanmar relations is multi-fold. Firstly, the warmer the ties, the chances of conspiracy to encircle and contain China, increases. Secondly, the easing of sanctions could open the floodgates for Western companies to return to Myanmar and invest graciously, creating strong competition for Chinese companies. In terms of regional influence, Beijing sees the USA as trying to economically replace China's leadership in the East and South East Asia. Specifically, China is more fearful that Myanmar's improved reputation and regional status might be exploited by the USA to advance its agenda at ASEAN on regional issues such as the South China Sea. Viewed from these perspectives, China's assessment of the U.S. presence in Myanmar is essentially a zero-sum. Any gains made by Washington will come at China's expense, either now or in the future.

China's Strategic Misjudging of Myanmar

After the 2010 elections, a large number of unexpected developments in Myanmar's domestic and foreign policy like freeing of political prisoners as well as lifting the ban on the domestic press revealed several basic wrong judgments by China in its strategic plan for Myanmar. Firstly, China totally underestimated the momentum of political reform and democratization within Myanmar. Prior to the 2010 elections, Chinese analysts had unilaterally concluded that the new civilian government would be in full control of the military as before. In their assessment, the newly-formed civilian government was clearly a military tactic to strengthen its legitimacy with no intention to give up power, but it proved the opposite. Secondly, domestic politics in Myanmar would remain the same and relations with the West would not improve in the long run. This too was a complete misjudgement. Besides, Beijing seemed to be ignorant of the anti-China sentiment in Myanmar. From China's perspective, public opinion in Myanmar did not matter much for China's interests as long as the military backed Chinese projects. Thirdly, China overestimated the political and economic influence on Myanmar. It thought that because it was the biggest investor in Myanmar and provider of critical international political shielding for Myanmar's military regime, China was sure of some privileges in Myanmar. With no removal of Western sanctions in sight, China was comfortably positioned for Myanmar's continued reliance on China. But the surprise came when the West lifted the sanctions from Myanmar and began to engage with its government.

Myanmar 2016: Rebalancing Relations with China

As the transition from being a military pariah nation to a quasi-democracy and finally to a full democracy continues, the government faces an uphill task of reshaping and rebalancing political, economic and strategic relations with neighbours, especially with China, its largest trading partner by far and a key source of FDI. The importance of the relationship was seen immediately after the new government of Myanmar took over office on 30 March 2016. The Chinese Foreign Minister Wang Yi visited Myanmar on 5 and 6 April 2016. China had ensured that he should be the first foreign dignitary to meet Aung San Suu Kyi. However, this was largely symbolic; no major outcomes were announced, including the controversial mega Myitsone dam project suspended by former President Thein Sein and which Suu Kyi said she had not yet been able to study in detail. Subsequently, Suu Kyi visited the USA in September, possibly before any visit to China—and her second major foreign trip, after Thailand in June—will no doubt be seen closely by China, especially given the long-standing concerns over her closeness to India and the West. Her only earlier visit to China was in June 2015 as NLD leader. Suspension of the $ 3.4 billion Myitsone Dam Project in 2011 had sent shockwaves in Beijing and marked the start of an era of re-engagement between Myanmar and the West. Though China is keen to restart construction, it understands that negative public opinion on this project in Myanmar may make it unfeasible. At the moment, it would be keen to protect its other major projects, in particular, development of a large port and SEZ on the coast at Kyaukpyu and extract a quid pro quo for any cancellation of the Myitsone project. China is also using its considerable leverage over armed ethnic groups in the border areas to show Myanmar that it has a direct influence on any process of resolving these issues that will require more than a project-specific guarantee and peace process reassurances. It will involve developing a broad, mutually-acceptable bond of cordial bilateral relations. A specially delicate aspect is enhanced military-to military cooperation between Myanmar and the West, something of significant interest to the Myanmar military as it seeks to broaden defence cooperation. It is of great importance that Western militaries in particular explore appropriate avenues. First, it is essential for sustainability of the transition that the military sees broad and sustainable benefits from its decision to give up political power. A driver of change has been the desire of Myanmar to build strategic relationships with the West, particularly the USA, and access high-quality military training. Secondly, socialisation of a new generation of officers with peers in democratic countries can make an important contribution to reform of the institution. The West will have to be extraordinarily careful on what kind of training it provides, since Myanmar's military is still involved in internal armed conflict and has a grim human rights record. Myanmar will need to ensure that it rises above being over-dependent on China and maintains just positive and constructive relations with Beijing.

5

INDIA–MYANMAR RELATIONS

On the day of Burma's independence on 4 January 1948, Prime Minister Jawaharlal Nehru had referred to the shared future awaiting both countries. *"As in the past, so in the future, the people of India will stand shoulder to shoulder with the people of Burma, and whether we have to share good fortune or ill fortune, we shall share it together. This is a great and solemn day not only for Burma, but for India, and for the whole of Asia,"* he said.

India and Myanmar share historical, ethnic, cultural and religious ties. In real terms, both countries share a 1643 kilometre-long land border. A large population of Indian origin, estimated to be 2.5 million, stays in Myanmar. Four north-eastern states—Arunachal Pradesh, Nagaland, Manipur and Mizoram—share their boundaries with Myanmar. India also shares the strategic waters of the Bay of Bengal, including the area of the strategically important Andaman and Nicobar islands where the two closest Indian and Myanmar's islands are barely 30 kilometres apart. Myanmar's ports provide India the shortest approach route to several of India's north-eastern states. As both countries emerged as sovereign nation-states out of the British Empire, India and Burma adhered to the five principles of peaceful co-existence formulated at the Bandung Conference in 1954 as the core of their foreign policies towards each other. These were:

(1) Mutual respect for each other's territorial integrity and sovereignty; (2) Mutual non-aggression; (3) Mutual non-interference in each other's internal affairs; (4) Equality and mutual benefit; and (5) Peaceful co-existence.

Both countries were also active in the Non-Aligned Movement. However, the military takeover and extreme socialist policies of the Gen Ne Win regime placed the relations in turbulence. This period saw large-scale nationalization of industries and repression of minorities. During the decade of the Sixties a large number of Indian settlers were expelled from Myanmar. By 1964 this figure had reached over 10000 refugees which did not go down well with the Indian government.

Myanmar was a province of British India until 1937, when it became a separate colony. Indian freedom movements had a profound impact on its political thinking, and its nationalist campaign was borrowed heavily from its Indian counterparts. The education, civil services and administrative structures were also strikingly similar.

But despite racial tensions within Myanmar, relations with India as a country were reasonably cordial after Myanmar gained freedom in 1948 and, indeed, throughout the Fifties. India was looked upon as a model socialist state for Myanmar's policies of neutrality and non-alignment. Their independence struggle hero, Gen Aung San, had consulted Pt. Jawaharlal Nehru both before and after his meetings with British Prime Minister Clement Attlee in London preceding independence. Aung San was assassinated on 19 July 1947, six months before the British left Burma on 4 January 1948, but his successor, U Nu, maintained close links with India as well. Following the military takeover in 1962, many of the remaining Indians had their property confiscated and forced to leave Burma, but this never clouded Indo-Burmese relations to any significant extent. Ne Win's new government, however, downgraded relations with India. Instead of being a neutral but friendly neighbour, India became more or less a non-entity in Burmese foreign policy. Ne Win's main concerns were directed towards China and the Chinese-supported communist insurgency which gained momentum a few years after his coup d'état in Rangoon.

India's policy of benign neglect changed dramatically after the bloody events of 1988. Along with all other major democracies in the world, India came out strongly in support of the pro-democracy movement, while China and the ASEAN (Association of Southeast Asian Nations) countries sided with the ruling military junta.

Period of Cordial Relations: 1948-1962

Burma's immediate problem after independence in 1948 was widespread insurgency in practically every part of the country. The CPB resorted to armed struggle. On 28 March, army units rose in mutiny, and Karen and Mon ethnic insurgents followed suit in 1949. U Nu's fledgling parliamentary government would most probably have fallen had it not been for massive support from Nehru in India. At the height of the civil war in 1950, both India and Britain provided Burma with 10,000 small weapons each and arranged with other Commonwealth countries, including Australia, Sri Lanka and Pakistan (Burma never joined the Commonwealth, though), to provide a loan of 6 million pounds sterling to tide the acute position of the state's treasury, until the insurgent forces could be suppressed.

A cordial relationship emerged as a result, and there were only two problems facing Indo-Burmese relations during the Fifties: independent Burma had inherited a disputed and undemarcated border with India, and a debt incurred during the colonial period while Burma was an Indian province. There was no urgency to solve either problem and not until 1953 did U Nu and Nehru personally inspect a disputed area in the Naga Hills. Burma's debt to India was also settled smoothly.

In 1954, India and Burma signed an agreement according to which Burma sold 900,000 tons of rice to India at a special low price and agreed to make payment toward the pension fund of civil servants of Indian origin that had been incurred when Burma was a part of India. Indo-Burmese relations throughout Burma's democratic period are perhaps best summed up by the Burmese prime minister of that era, U Nu: "I was at one with Pandit Nehru in the observance of the principles of peaceful coexistence. We believed in the democratic way of life and in the policy of strict neutrality...there was nothing to disturb the relations between the two countries that their leaders had worked hard to foster."

Period of Indifference: 1962-1988

The nature of Indo-Burmese relations changed after Ne Win's coup d'état in March 1962, albeit gradually, in a process of attrition rather than because of any decision made by policy makers in New Delhi. After a few years in power, Ne Win's new 'Revolutionary Council' decided to nationalize privately-owned businesses and factories in a process that is referred by many authors as 'Burmese Socialism.' Thousands of people lost their livelihood and since there was little prospect of employment in the new state-owned economy that emerged, many were compelled to leave for India. No compensation was given and all Indians leaving the country were allowed to take out only Kyats 75 per adult, Kyats 15 for each child, and Kyats 250 worth of jewellery. During the period 1964-68, some 150,000 Indo-Burmese left Burma, many of whom were Burmese, not Indian citizens. The Indian community in Burma appealed to the Indian government for help. New Delhi sent a representative to investigate but he concluded that the policy was an internal Burmese affair. India did not protest.

But relations between India and Burma did deteriorate after the 1962 coup d'état in Rangoon. Trade and cultural exchanges were reduced to a minimum, mainly because of lack of interest from Burma. Until 1962, many young Burmese had come to India to study, both at private schools in the hills (Darjeeling, Nainital, etc.) and in Indian universities in Kolkata, Mumbai and Delhi. But the number of Burmese students declined considerably after 1962. Burma went into a state of self-imposed isolation; relations with India were no longer important.

The only bilateral issue that remained to be discussed was the common border and in the Seventies, the fact that Naga and Mizo insurgents from India's north-east maintained sanctuaries in remote hill areas of western and north-western Burma, areas that were not controlled by the central government in Rangoon. From these cross-border sanctuaries, the insurgents launched occasional raids into India just to retreat into Burma again, beyond the reach of India's security forces.

On 10 March 1967, Burma and India agreed on the common border and an agreement was signed. The ethnic unrest in India's north-east, on the other hand, spilled across the border into Burma in the early Sixties and since then India's main concern in Burma has been insurgency. Indeed, until 1988, India cared little about anything else in Burma. Successive Indian army offensives against Naga rebels on the Indian side of the border had weakened tribal resistance inside India. In 1963, General Kaito, a commander of the Naga rebel army, established a base in the Somra tract in Burma, opposite Manipur's Ukhrul district. At the same time, some Burmese Nagas—distant cousins of the Indian Nagas—were beginning to show an interest in the insurgency. S.S. Khaplang, a Naga from Burma's Sagaing division, set up the Eastern Naga Revolutionary Council (ENRC) in 1965, and cooperated closely with the Naga National Council (NNC) in India. The Burmese army, preoccupied with fighting more important insurgencies elsewhere in the country, showed scant interest in this alliance while the Indian Nagas were establishing more permanent bases inside Burma, well beyond reach of the army. From India's point of view, the situation became even more alarming when groups of Nagas began trekking though northern Burma to China where they received military training, arms and ammunition. Equipped with modern weapons, these Nagas returned to India, where fierce battles were fought with the Indian armed forces. This was during the decade 1968-78, when China gave all-out support to the Communist Party of Burma (CPB) and other insurgencies in Burma, notably the ethnic Kachin Independence Army (KIA), whose troops often escorted the Nagas on their way to China. In 1980, 200 Indian troops and 400 Burmese soldiers attacked a Naga base in the Upper Sagaing division and in the following year Indian troops crossed the border and bombarded the then Naga headquarters at Mongkhwe, also in north western Sagaing division. An unofficial agreement apparently existed between the Indians and the Burmese according to which troops from either country could cross up to 10 miles inside each other's territory "in hot pursuit of insurgents."

In a way, this was a major concession to India, since only India was keen to destroy the Naga base in Burma and only Indian troops were inclined to take advantage of the agreement. An enthusiastic local press in Nagaland declared "India is at last getting effective help from the Burmese government in dealing with the Naga rebels who have been enjoying sanctuary across the border."

The euphoria was, however, short-lived. Burma paid no further attention to the Naga problem and relations with India did not significantly improve. In 1982, the Burmese government promulgated a new citizenship act according to which full citizenship would only be given to people who could prove that their ancestors had lived in Burma prior to the First Anglo-Burmese War in 1824-26. 'Non-indigenous races' such as the Indo-Burmese and the Sino-Burmese were immediately affected. Many lost their full Burmese citizenship and were officially demoted to second-class citizens.

Period of Breaking Frigidity: 1988-2010

The 1988 uprising for democracy became a turning point in Indo-Burmese relations. India was among the first countries to comment on the Burmese crisis. On 10 September 1988, when millions of people were marching for democracy in virtually every town and city in Burma and more than a week before the army stepped in and suppressed the protests New Delhi expressed its support for "the undaunted resolve of the Burmese people to achieve their democracy." Later, when thousands of dissidents fled the bloody crackdown that resulted from the military takeover on 18 September, India became the only neighbour that adopted a clear-cut refugee policy. On 25 October, India's then External Affairs Minister, P.V. Narasimha Rao, told a parliamentary panel that "strict instructions have been issued not to turn back any genuine Burmese refugee seeking shelter in India."

After the 1990s, when the world shunned the military regime of Myanmar due to incessant human rights abuses, China not only became its key ally but also its main arms supplier. It supplied arms amounting to USD 1.4 billion in 1989 followed by another deal of USD 400 million in 1994 which proved to be a shot in the arm for the waning military prowess of *Tatmadaw*. However, after the 2011 elections and establishment of a democratic government under President Thein Sein which brought about revolutionary reforms, the USA, and countries of the EU seemed to be moving in swiftly to re-establish the snapped ties. Recently, the United Kingdom invited 30 Myanmar officers to a prestigious defence conference. Australia is also pledging basic military engagement to support security sector reforms. The USA wants to restart defence training for Myanmar that was halted 25 years ago after a ruthless crackdown on protesters in 1988. It must be remembered that before the sanctions were applied, the USA had financed USD 4.7 million in military sales between 1980 and 1988 and trained 167 officers at American military schools under the International Military Education and Training (IMET), a program jointly managed by the State Department and Defence Department that helps more than 120 countries. Even today, the IMET alumni occupy some important positions in the military hierarchy.

India's position vis-a-vis other developed nations is unique, as it not only shares common historical ties but also 1,643 kilometres of border. Due to its rugged terrain, the border management can only be effective if both nations assiduously cooperate. The problem of the border gets compounded because of some insurgent groups that are known to seek safe havens across the border when chased by Indian armed forces. And tranquillity on the border is a prime concern of both the countries. Good military ties with our eastern neighbour means better border management and better control over insurgent groups operating in the Northeast. It also strengthens bilateral ties with the present Chair of the ASEAN community of nations.

Period of Mutual Trust: 2010–till date

After the success of the 2010 election, Thein Sien took over as President of Myanmar. And in the 2011 by-elections the NLD won 44 out of 45 seats where the party fielded candidates. Aung San Suu Kyi was among those elected. This gave a new fillip to the democratic process in the country. The USA and a number of European countries began to ease the sanctions. India too immediately moved on the path of further improving relations. The visit of Indian Prime Minister Manmohan Singh to Myanmar in May 2012 was a watershed in the relations and it paved the way to further strengthen the ties and laid the foundation of bilateral economic cooperation. This was followed by the visit of Defence Minister A.K. Antony in January 2013 and visits by the Naval and Air Chiefs. As a result of the improved relations both the nations conducted their first ever joint naval exercise in March 2013. Undoubtedly, India has to counter China's strategic moves in the region and the time has come when India must assist Myanmar to augment not only its military equipment but also provide training to its armed forces.

Towards this end, India had agreed to assist Myanmar in building Offshore Patrol Vehicles (OPVs) in Indian dockyards and also train its pilots on Russian MI-35 helicopters. India had supplied four Islander maritime patrol aircraft and naval gunboats and some 105-mm light artillery guns, mortars, grenade-launchers and rifles. But Myanmar has asked for much more equipment including radars, sensors and sonars for its naval frigates and corvettes.

The visit by the army chief from October 29 to November 1, 2013 is important because of its timing and also because of the bridges it built at that time. It seemed that China became vary of the growing visits of Indian and Western dignitaries and sent its deputy chairman of the Chinese Central Military Commission (CMC), Gen Fan Changlong, to meet President Thein Sein and the Myanmar Army Chief, Senior General Min Hlaing, in October that year. Aung Kyaw Zaw, a Myanmar military and political analyst commented in '*The Irrawaddy*' that he believed Fan Changlong also represented the Chinese Communist Party during his trip to Myanmar. He said

Beijing's concerns over Myanmar's growing military ties with the USA and the United Kingdom could have motivated the visit. "China is very much concerned about relations between the Burmese army and major international countries," he said. The visit of the Indian Army Chief at this point of time not only bolstered the growing proximity between the two nations but commenced the build-up of much-needed military ties between the two armies. Gen Bikram Singh held talks with President Thein Sen, Foreign Minister U Wunna Maung Lwin and the Commander-in-Chief of the defence services, Senior General Min Aung Hlaing, among others. He also gave two war game software packages called 'Combat decision resolution' and 'Infantry company commanders tactical trainer' which have been customized for training for the Myanmarese Army. He also gave five gliders for the Defence Services Academy at Pwin Oo Lwin. Another gesture was to incorporate Myanmarese armed forces special training packages in the Indian Army's counter-insurgency and jungle warfare school at Vairengte in Mizoram.

The second half of 2012 saw the historic visits of Aung San Suu Kyi and President Thein Sein to Washington and this was followed by a short reciprocal visit by President Barak Obama at Yangon on November 19, 2012. This historic visit not only endorsed U.S. acceptance but opened the flood gates for further reforms and aid. Speaking to students at Yangon University during his six-hour tour, he said, "Today I've come to keep my promise and extend the hand of friendship. Reforms launched from the top of society must meet the aspirations of citizens who form its foundation. The flickers of progress that we have seen must not be extinguished." He later met President Thein Sein and main opposition leader Aung San Suu Kyi.

India's Look East Policy

India adopted its famous 'Look East Policy' in the early Nineties. The policy involved engaging with the countries of Southeast Asia. The next few years saw a number of visits exchanged by dignitaries from India and Myanmar. India, while still supportive of the pro-democracy movement, began to actively engage with the military *junta* and tried to revive old ties. However, the road was not easy as the Chinese had already made huge investments in almost every sector. Shyam Saran, the former Indian Ambassador to Myanmar in 1997, had said that "the relations were still frigid." In November 2000, Gen Maung Aye, the second-most prominent leader of Myanmar's military *junta*, led a high-power delegation including Deputy Prime Minister Lt. Gen. Tin Hla along with a team of ministers to New Delhi. The then Indian Home Minister, L.K. Advani, tried to break the frigidity and talked about warming of ties between the two countries. This visit was followed by a six-day visit of Gen Than Shwe to New Delhi in 2004 and in 2006 by President Abdul Kalam's visit to Yangon. During these visits, a number of bilateral treaties were signed relating to sharing of cultural, social, technological and military cooperation. Subsequent years saw the Government of India's active involvement in over a dozen projects in Myanmar, both in infrastructural and non-infrastructural areas. These include upgradation and resurfacing of the 160-kilometre long Tamu-Kalewa-Kalemyo road; construction and upgradation of the Rhi-Tiddim road in Myanmar and the mega Rs. 1,500 crore Kaladan Multimodal transport project.

The Kaladan Multimodal transport project will link the north-eastern states via the Bay of Bengal and Myanmar route. An ADSL project for high-speed data link in 32 Myanmar cities has been completed by TCIL. The ONGC, GAIL and ESSAR are participants in the energy sector in Myanmar. RITES is involved in development of the rail transportation system and in the supply of railway coaches, locomotives and spare parts. In September 2008, NHPC signed an agreement for development of the Tamanthi and Shwezaye Hydro-Electric Power project on Chindwin River. A heavy turbo-truck assembly plant set up in Myanmar by TATA Motors with GOI financial assistance was inaugurated on December 31, 2010.

Other projects include revamping of the Ananda Temple in Bagan (project cost $3 million), upgradation of the Yangon Children's Hospital and Sittwe General Hospital(project cost $7 million). India has also assisted in the reconstruction of a high school and six primary schools in Tarlay township, the area worst affected by the severe earthquake that struck north-eastern Myanmar in March 2011.

Restored Ananda Bagan Temple

Yangon Children and Sittwe General Hospital

However, what needs to be kept in mind by Indian industry and the Government is the wider interest of the north eastern states so that the dividends of growth are seen on both sides of the border. A proper roadmap of government-industry should include sectors that not only give inclusive growth to Myanmar but also regional growth for our eastern states. The invitation to invest in the oil and energy sector by President Thein Sein must be utilized by the Government post haste keeping in mind that China has already completed the Shwe gas pipeline and made it functional also. We must think in terms of harnessing the energy reserves in Myanmar and also create some energy-processing hubs in the eastern states for subsequent use in the development of the adjoining areas. Setting up of ancillary industries to supply specific projects in Myanmar can also be planned and some economic zones can be specified for such purpose. The proposals must also stress upon the development of road and communications infrastructure to support the projects undertaken through the land route. A proper planning of the projects can have a long-term impact on development for both the economies; Myanmar and Northeast India. It is time for us to reframe our 'Look-East' policy to make it into 'Look-East through North-East.'

High-level visits have been a regular feature of India-Myanmar relations for several years and it increased after the new government came to power in 2010. President Thein Sein paid a State visit to India on October 12-15, 2011 and had a meeting with the Prime Minister of India, Dr. Manmohan Singh, which was followed by delegation-level talks. President Thein Sein was accompanied by Chief of General Staff Lt Gen Hla Htay Win and 11 Union Ministers and one Union Deputy Minister and senior officials. In December 2011, the Speaker of Pyithu Hluttaw (Lower House) Thura U Shwe Mann led a high-level parliamentary delegation to India. The objective was to share India's experience in parliamentary practices and procedures. Myanmar Foreign Minister U Wunna Maung Lwin paid an official visit to India from January 22-26, 2012. These were finally followed by Prime Minister Dr. Manmohan Singh's visit to Myanmar in May 2012. This was the first visit of an Indian prime minister in 25 years. During the visit, several new initiatives were announced and 12 MoUs were signed and many agreements including extension of a new line of credit (LOC) worth USD 500 million were inked.

From 'Look East' to 'Act East' Policy

India's 'Look East' policy (LEP) was introduced in the early and mid 1990s by the then prime minister P.V. Narasimha Rao. Subsequently, it was endorsed by Indian Prime Ministers Atal Bihari Vajpayee and Manmohan Singh. During the ASEAN meet in June 2015, Prime Minister Narendra Modi told the world leaders that his government accorded high priority to turn India's erstwhile 'Look East' policy into an 'Act East' policy.

It should be noted with credence that since coming to power in

2014, the government of Narendra Modi has lent India's 'Look East' policy even greater momentum leading to unveiling of an upgraded 'Act East Policy' during the India-ASEAN Summit in Myanmar in November 2014. This gives a clear message that India is becoming increasingly willing to play a more active and prominent strategic role in East and Southeast Asia. It goes beyond doubt that Myanmar is the 'door to ASEAN' for trade and strategic depth. Modi's three-day visit to Myanmar brought ASEAN and Myanmar back on the Indian focus. The shift from LEP to AEP does not merely show a departure from LEP but a 'commitment' to implementation of the projects.

The important aspect of the visit was the focus given to the three C's—Culture, Commerce and Connectivity. Tourism is one of the important aspects of cultural sharing and religious tourism of the Buddhist circuit like linking Bodh Gaya to Yangon would act as a boost to increase people-to-people contact between India and Myanmar.

On the commerce aspect the India-ASEAN Free Trade Agreement has already been made operational and includes both services and investments. On the issue of connectivity, there is an urgent need to move forward with the plans that have been in the pipeline. The completion of the Tamu-Kalewa-Kalemyo sector of the India-Myanmar-Thailand Trilateral Highway is poised to create a new dynamic in India's multi-faceted ties with the region. Whilst both Myanmar and India are focusing on the development of the border regions, these projects will act as vital catalysts to deliver on the proposed outcomes.

In order to provide an accurate strategic foresight of Indo-Myanmar relations and its implications for India, it is necessary to understand the historical and present context, national ambitions and the current means available to achieve these goals. The period of the next five to ten years, from an Indian standpoint, will be one of balancing between securing its economic investment through bilateral relations with the new government which has come into power after the 2015 election. India in its earnest quest to improve relations with

Myanmar is likely to give a stiff challenge not only to China but also to the other Western countries. Also, China will have to face growing resentment of local Chinese presence in Myanmar; border instability; weak Myanmar governance; and stronger international commitments.

Alternatively, amidst the military *junta's* controversial history, it wants to prove to the regional and international community that it is a legitimate government elected by the people. Through the Seven Step Roadmap to Democracy and the election in 2015, the *junta* wants to show its credibility as the government of Myanmar.

In the earlier period, the *junta* was successful in making regional actors compete for its natural resources and its strategic importance works in its favour. When China, India and ASEAN compete for access to Myanmar, they are supporting the *junta* financially, which gets translated into political support. Also, the *junta* does not want direct foreign involvement in its national affairs. India's policy being less assertive is more conducive to Myanmar's objectives.

Kaladan Multimodal Transit Transport Project (KMTTP)

In April 2008, the Indian Government headed by the Dr Manmohan Singh signed an agreement with the Myanmar regime for development of the Kaladan Multi-Modal Transit Transport Project which is also known as the Kaladan Project. The project will connect Eastern Indian sea ports, particularly Kolkata port, with Sittwe port at a total distance of 593 kilometres. It will then link Sittwe to land-locked Mizoram in Northeast India via the Kaladan river and road transport.

The project will be completed in three phases:

> Phase 1: Development of Sittwe port to handle the future increase in shipping levels. This includes the expansion of its seaport and the construction of a new inland waterway terminal. This entails deep dredging of the approach channel and the port area to facilitate 6,000-ton ships, as well as constructing two jetties and extensive loading and storage facilities that will significantly expand Sittwe's current

size and capacity. A larger jetty (219 metres × 15 metres) will be capable of handling 20,000-ton ocean freighters and a 54 metres × 15 metres inland waterway terminal jetty will cater to smaller vessels that ply in the Kaladan river. At present, Sittwe's port consists of a 78 metres × 15 metres jetty and is appropriate for vessels of 2,000-3,000 tons.

Phase 2: Deep dredging of 225 kilometres of the Kaladan river between Sittwe and Setpyitpyin (Kaletwa) in Chin State where another terminal will be built.

Phase 3: Construction of a 62 kilometre-long road connecting Setpyitpyin (Kaletwa) with Mizoram.

As per the initial plan, the first and second phases of the project were to begin by 2009. However, construction started in November 2010. The development of phases 1 and 2 for Sittwe port, the river dredging and the IWT at Kaletwa, were executed by the Inland Waterways Authority of India (IWAI) with Essar Projects Ltd. But the third phase of highway construction will be undertaken by Myanmar. The construction of the highway from Paletwa to the India-Myanmar border was originally to start from 2011-2012; however, the construction has not yet commenced. The entire project is planned to be completed in three years (2014-2016), with work suspended for five to six months of the year due to the monsoon.

Due to the challenging and technical difficulty of dredging small islands and rocks, especially in the upper part of the Kaladan river, the second and third phases have had to be altered: dredging of 225 kilometres of the Kaladan river between Sittwe and Setpyitpyin (Kaletwa) has been reduced to 158 kilometres between Sittwe and Paletwa, where another IWT terminal is being built to transfer cargo from river to road transport. As a result, the construction of the highway has to be extended from 62 kilometres to 129 kilometres between Paletwa in Burma's Chin State and the Mizoram border of India.

The project is going to be completely piloted and funded by the Ministry of External Affairs. The preliminary feasibility studies such as hydrographical surveys, etc., were carried out by the state-run Rail India Technical and Economic Services (RITES). However, no open and clear transparency regarding these studies has been made public. The development of Sittwe port and Kaladan waterway is expected to cost USD 68.24 million and the highway construction between Kaletwa and the Indian border is expected to be around USD 49.14 million. According to the April 2008 Framework, the Government of the Union of Myanmar will provide the required land and security for the project, including for personnel and technicians, free.

The Indian government will bear the full cost of the project which was originally estimated at USD 120 million (Rs 586 crore). After completion, the project will be handed over to the Myanmar government on the terms and conditions mutually agreed upon in the April 2008 Framework Agreement. These terms and conditions are outlined in two supplementary documents; however, they have not yet been made public. It is anticipated that Myanmar will take full ownership of the transport system but it will primarily be used by Indian companies to increase trade with Southeast Asia and links to the land-locked Mizoram region. It is expected, however, that few local citizens will use the Kaladan, since they will not be able to afford the tolls that the Myanmar government will impose on vessels using the waterway.

In October 2015, the Indian government approved the revised cost estimate of the Kaladan project from Rs 1,500 crore to Rs 2,904 crore.

To bolster ties with Myanmar, the Inland Waterways Authority of India has entered into an agreement with India Ports Global Private for a Rs 476-crore project to facilitate connectivity and trade. A memorandum of understanding (MoU) was signed between IWAI and IPGPL on June 1 for projects worth Rs 476 crore.

In 1992, following the breakdown of the Soviet Union, the Indian government launched its 'Look East Policy,' which, in the words of the then prime minister was, "a strategic shift in India's vision of the world and India's place in the evolving global economy."

From then on, a number of initiatives have been put in place to increase ties, largely in trade relations between India, members of the Association of Southeast Asian Nations (ASEAN) and other Asian states. As India's gateway to East Asia, the Myanmar's regime found itself in a key geo-strategic position, giving it a strong card in negotiations with India before the agreement on the Kaladan.

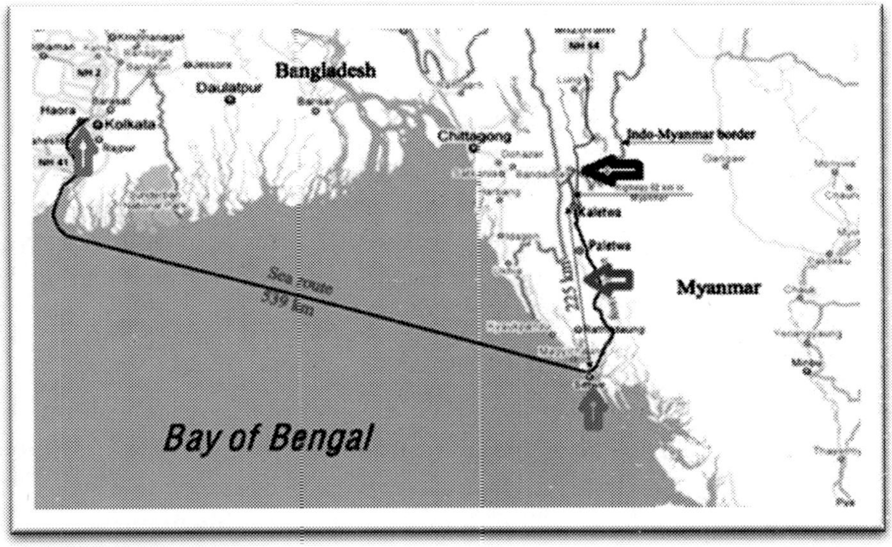

Source: www.gktoday.in

India's relationship with Myanmar is also largely based on a need to counter China's influence in the region and to deal directly with ASEAN countries. China has recently become Myanmar's second largest foreign investor and has built its own port in Kyaukphyu, just about 40 kilometres from Sittwe. The Kaladan project will secure India's Northeast with an alternate route for trade and transport.

Once completed, it will give a fillip to the ties between India and Myanmar. Moreover, the overall development of India's Northeast region and particularly land-locked states like Mizoram, will be greatly enhanced. Bilateral trade meetings were held between Myanmar trade and investment delegates and trade ministers from the four Northeastern Indian states in mid-September 2010 in an attempt to strengthen the ongoing trade between the two neighbours, particularly on the border.

The Kaladan project is likely to open up the economy of the region of the northeastern states in India and will connect to the Asian highway in the future, and thus open new trade routes.

Kaladan River

Kaladan is the longest and most used river, connecting Rakhine and Chin States. Approximately 350 kilometres in length, it originates from the hills in Mizoram and then flows through a narrow valley in the mountains of Chin State, descending to the Kaladan river that is the primary source of water and transport, irrigation and fishing for those living in the area. "We will find it really difficult for our daily survival if the river is blocked with larger vessels and dredged," said a villager.

Potential Impacts of the Project

Approximately about a million civilians live in townships along the Kaladan river. The large majority makes a living by fishing and farming and relies primarily on this river. Because of the lack of a road network, civilians living in the area rely on this waterway.

If the developments entailed by the Kaladan project take its course, many people may have to change their means of livelihood without any compensation from either government. The developments along this river and around Sittwe port area will permanently block access to fishing areas along the coast. When the residents are not able to access and use the river as before, the travel and transportation of goods for trade will be almost impossible.

Furthermore, the ecosystem of the area on which locals depend will be devastated causing a rapid decrease in food supplies in regions that are already highly food deficient. Seeing the overall picture, the construction of the Sittwe port and the waterway is going to help the local people.

In November 2010, the construction of Sittwe port was started. However, it received a lot of local complaints because of the sand that was being transported from Sittwe's beach to be placed in the port area. Worse still, construction of the port disturbed patients in Sittwe's general hospital and business along the bank of the river on Strand

Road where buildings began to crack due to the impact of port construction. Furthermore, people along the Strand Road remain concerned that their houses, shops and restaurants will be removed.

Progress of the Project

The progress of this project has been rather slow, owing to the tardiness of the governments and also due to the agitation by the locals who claim that there will be widespread environmental damage if this project is implemented. The work on the project is on. A memorandum of understanding (MoU) was signed between IWAI and IPGPL on June 1 for projects worth Rs 476 crore. Under this MoU, the work on the project includes developing a container depot at Sittwe and Paletwa and operations and maintenance of the completed work. Overall, IWAI shall remain as the overall PDC to MEA for implementation of the port and the IWT component of the Kaladan project.

Other Developmental Projects Undertaken by India are as follows:

1. **Tamu Kale Kalewa (TKK) Road** (US$ 27 Million) This vital 'Friendship' Road connects Moreh in Manipur to Tamu and onto to Kalemyo and Kalewa in Sagaing Region of Myanmar and is an important road for border trade. The upgradation of the 160 km road in Myanmar was taken up in 1997 and completed in 2001. Border Roads Organization (BRO) was the implementing agency. A small stretch of 28 km of the Kyigone-Kalewa stretch needs upgradation and is being assessed for execution. (Cost of the project is based on 2001 rates which factored for current cost of construction would amount to Approx. US$ 250 million at present value)
2. **Industrial Training Centre, Pakokku & Industrial Training Centre, Myingyan** (US$ 6 million)
   Government of India, through the Hindustan Machine Tools International Ltd (HMTI), assisted the Government of Myanmar in establishing two Vocational Training Centres at Pakokku and Myingyan (of a total of 6 such Centres which

exist) in Myanmar. HMTI has supplied the equipment and conducted training on site as well as in India. The ITCs provide vocational training on various industrial subjects including Machinist-Fitter, Machinist- Turner/ Miller, Tools and Die Making, CNC machinists, Industrial Electrician, Electronic Mechanic, Sheet Metal and Welding Worker and Foundry. While the Pakokku Centre was handed over in 2011; the Myingyan Centre was handed over to the Government of Myanmar in October 2013.

3. **India-Myanmar Center for Enhancement of Information Technology Skills (IMCEITS)** (US$ 0.3 Million)

   Government of India supported the establishment of the IMCEITS, to assist Myanmar, in its endeavour to provide short term courses on Software and Application Programming for eligible Myanmar students, with an aim to further refine the IT 'skills' of the population. IMCEITS was established through C-DAC in 2010.

4. **Myanmar-India Entrepreneurship Development Centre** (MIEDC) (US$ 0.3 Million)

   MIEDC was established at the Institute of Economics (Hlaing Campus) Yangon in 2009 as part of the Initiative for ASEAN

Integration (IAI) programme. The Entrepreneurship Development Institute of India (EDII) implemented the project through supply of equipment, development of courseware and also deploying an Advisor stationed for 4 years, till 2013. Under its training programme, the Centre has conducted 25 courses for 1310 participants in 2012-2013, imparting training to 3000 participants since its establishment. The Centre conducts courses on a wide range of popular themes including entrepreneurship appreciation/ sensitization programmes, capacity building of NGOs, development of training manuals for SMEs/Exports/micro Enterprises, women empowerment and project evaluation, appraisal, research and development.

5. **Myanmar-India Centre for English Language Training** (MICELT) (US$ 0.1 million)

MICELT was set up under the Initiative for Asian Integration (IAI) programme in 2009 at the Yangon University with an aim of providing a permanent venue for teaching and raising the general level of proficiency in English language in Myanmar. The project was implemented by the English Foreign Language University (EFLU) Hyderabad thorugh deployment of faculty and equipment. MICELT operates under the Ministry of Education, Myanmar and

shares its staff with the English Language Department of Yangon University. Till date, 18 courses on English proficiency have been conducted between 2009-2013, for a total of 844 participants. Courses are generally conducted for Myanmar Civil Servants and officials of various Ministries of Myanmar. Special courses are conducted for journalists, businessmen, law enforcement officers and English language trainers as per demand.

India–Myanmar Economic and Trade Ties

Owing to the opening up of Myanmar's economy in the last three years, its condition has shown tremendous improvement. Its real GDP growth has shown reasonable improvement of 4.7 per cent in 2008 to 5.5 per cent in 2013 and is likely to touch 6.2 per cent in 2014. Its overall exports too have grown from USD 8.11 billion in 2011-2012 to 8.9 billion in 2012-2013. Indian industry is showing an increasing interest in Myanmar. As per the Ministry of External Affairs (MEA) report, India-Myanmar trade has grown exponentially in the last few years. From a meagre USD 12.4 million in 1980-1981 to USD 1,070.88 million in 2010-2011, $ 1.87 billion in 2011-2012 and $ 1.98 billion in 2012-13, and $2 billion in 2014, it is likely to touch $ 3 billion by 2018. India accounted for 15 per cent of Myanmar's global exports in 2012 and was ranked as the second largest export market after Thailand which is at 41 per cent while China was at 14 per cent. However, as far as Myanmar's imports were concerned, India's share was a meagre 3 per cent with China at 37 per cent and Thailand at 20 per cent. India generally maintains a trade deficit with Myanmar which has increased from $ 293 million in 2001 to $ 860 in 2012-2013. India's imports from Myanmar are dominated by agricultural items (beans, pulses and forest-based products form 90 per cent of our imports). India's main exports to Myanmar are primary and semi-finished steel and pharmaceuticals, machinery, electrical and electronic equipment, etc.

In December 2012, President Thein Sein made a special visit to India and his closed-door meeting with members of the CII (along with representatives of the government) at Mumbai assumes significance in terms of investment opportunities and also for India's strategic interests in the region. He invited India's industry captains to invest in agriculture, energy and infrastructure. The CII has reciprocated Thein Sein's gesture by proposing five points of connectivity between the two countries in culture and commerce; promoting integration and synergy in power and railway sectors; appropriate banking arrangements to foster trade and investment; enhancing bilateral engagement in trade protection, and co-operation and collaboration in industries like tourism and software. In June 2013, India and Myanmar agreed to take the ambit of trade to include textiles, infrastructure, oil and gas. India's Commerce and Industry Minister Anand Sharma visited Myanmar in June 2013 and offered India's commitment to help Myanmar in strengthening the banking system as we inherit common banking laws. At present, India is the fourth largest trade partner of Myanmar after China, Thailand and Singapore. (*Source*: CII)

After the reforms initiated by the government, Myanmar's economy is fast showing rejuvenation. Many new opportunities for bilateral trade and investment have emerged and, as a result, Myanmar's GDP is expected to increase from 5.5 per cent in 2013 to 6.2 per cent in 2014. Myanmar's global trade has also seen an almost four-fold rise from $ 5.6 billion in 2003 to $ 25 billion in 2012.

Recent large projects bagged by Indian companies

a) Punj Lloyd – US$ 475 million (oil and gas pipeline)
b) L&T (Zawtika) – US$ 250 million (well-head platforms and pipelines);
c) Jubilant Energy – PSC-I Block);
d) L&T (Yetagun) – US$ 112 million (Wellhead platform & pipelines);
e) Nipha Exports – US$ 20 million (Multiple vegetable oil processing complex);
f) Vihan Networks Ltd. – US$ 5 million (Mobile telecom);

Source: India-Myanmar Strategic Partnership Seminar by RIS, 4 Feb 2013.

Table 1: India-Myanmar Bilateral Trade (in million US$)

Figures in brackets indicate variation from previous year(s)

Year	*2011-12*	*2012-13*	*2013-14*	*2014- 15*	*2015-16*
India's exports	**545.38** *(70.1%)*	**544.66** *(-0.13%)*	**787.01** *(44.5%)*	**773.74** *(-1.69)*	**1068.20** *(38.15%)*
India's imports	**1,381.15** *(35.72%)*	**1,412.69** *(2.28%)*	**1395.67** *(-1.20%)*	**1231.54** *(-11.76)*	**984.27** *(-20.08%)*
Total Trade	**1,870.20** *(39.75%)*	**1,957.35** *(1.6%)*	**2182.68** *(11.51)*	**2005.28** *(-8.13)*	**2052.47** *(2.38%)*

Source: DGFT, Dept of Commerce, India.

Table 2: India's major Imports from Myanmar (in million US$)

	Category / Items Group	*2013-14*	*2014-15*	*2015-16*
1	Pulses and beans	624.13	813.85	819.91
2	Wood & articles	748.74	382.12	125.03
3	Fish, meat & preparations	2.90	5.37	4.21
4	Other edible items	14.82	26.27	31.56
5	Animal or vegetable fats and oils	2.91	0.88	0.11
6	Mineral Fuels, Mineral Oils and Products of their Distillation; Bituminous substances; Mineral waxes	0.22	0.49	0
7	Inorganic and Organic Chemicals	0.02	0	0.73
8	boilers, machinery and mechanical appliances	0.08	0.41	0.13
9	Electrical Machinery and Equipment and parts	0.41	0.11	0.08
10	Iron and Steel (Articles of Iron and Steel)	0.01	0	0.10
11	Raw Hide & Skins	0.38	1.31	0.67
12	Plastic and Articles thereof	0	0	0.02
13	Rubber and Articles thereof	0.15	0.45	0.18
14	Miscellaneous	0.9	0.28	1.54
	Total	1395.67	1231.54	984.27

Source: DGFT, Dept of Commerce, India.

Table 3: India's major Exports to Myanmar (in million US$)

	Category / Items Group	*2013-14*	*2014-15*	*2015-16*
1	Sugars & Sugar Confectionery	8.52	0.55	457.09
2	Pharmaceuticals	137.19	169.17	152.23
3	Electrical Machinery & Equipment	82.16	124.87	73.46
4	Boiler, Machinery & parts	133.99	76.09	46.07
5	Iron & steel	104.27	74.74	30.43
6	Residues waste from the food industry	60.77	48.9	19.33

	Category / Items Group	2013-14	2014-15	2015-16
7	Cotton & yarn	56.19	46.91	49.50
8	Vehicles other than railway	32.55	44.39	37.52
9	Miscellaneous	39.55	41.74	75.77
10	Garment & textiles	15.54	30.62	39.33
11	Other metals & articles	21.61	21.02	20.43
12	Chemicals & allied products	14.99	18.27	20.43
13	Tools, implements	5.39	17.33	4.04
14	Edible items	17.31	17.03	15.53
15	Rubber & articles	12.89	10.54	7.65
16	Dairy Produce	13.68	10.2	0.11
17	Earths & stone, lime & cement	9.42	9.11	1.4
18	Plastic & articles	2.76	7.22	14.39
19	Minerals oils	8.09	3.93	2.94
20	Locomotives, rolling stock & parts	9.97	1.11	0.55
21	Fertilizer	0.17	0	0
	Total	**787.01**	**773.74**	**1068.20**

Source: DGFT, Dept of Commerce, India.

Border Trade

A very important part of the relationship between the two countries is the commencement of border trade. It started with the Border Trade Agreement signed on 21 Jan 1994 between India and Myanmar (annexure 1). Trade actually commenced from 12 April 1995 at one border post, Moreh, in Manipur. Under this agreement, trade is currently carried out through three designated border points, one each in Manipur, Mizoram and Nagaland. The agreement accords a formal sanction to informal border trade between the two countries. It holds importance in promoting economic ties between the two countries. Initially, the agreement provided for cross-border trade in 22 products, mainly agricultural products, and was increased to 40 commodities in 2008. The list was further augmented to 62 items in 2012. The latest items include agricultural machinery, bicycles, coal, electric appliances, fabricated steel products, etc.

The border trade was USD 12 million in 2012-2013, which was much less when compared with Myanmar-China and Myanmar-Thailand border trades. Two border trade points, Moreh-Tamu (1995) and Zowkhathar-Rhi (2004) have been operationalized so far with an agreement on a third trade point, Avakhung-Leshi, concluded recently.

However lack of infrastructure on both sides of the border remains a major limitation to augment border trade.

In 2013-2014, overall Myanmar recorded a 58 per cent hike in its overall border trade with USD 3.367 billion; however, India-Myanmar border trade in that period amounted to USD 45 million only. Subsequently due to efforts made by the Government of India in 2016-2017, this border trade almost doubled at USD 87 million.

Table 4: Trends of Bilateral Border Trade (in million US$)

Year	*Myanmar exports*	*Myanmar Imports*	*Total trade*	*Balance of Trade*
2012-2013	8.857	3.17	12.027	5.687
2013-2014	27.971	17.164	45.135	10.807
2014-2015	42.613	18.113	60.726	24.50
2015-2016	53.027	18.617	71.644	34.41
2016-2017	63.461	24.435	87.896	39.026
2017 (April–Sept)	26.910	6.823	33.733	20.087

Source: Ministry of Commerce, Myanmar.

Permissible Items for Border Trade Between India-Myanmar

Under this agreement total of 62 commodities, have been approved for trade across India-Myanmar border (Annexure II). These are as follows:

- **22 commodities/items notified by Public Notice No. 289(PN)/92-97 dated 10th April, 1995:** Bamboo, Betel Nuts and Leaves, Chilies, Coriander Seeds, Food Items for Local consumption, Fresh Vegetables, Fruits, Garlic, Ginger, Katha, Minor forest products (excluding Teak), Mustard/Rape seed, Onion, Pulses and Beans, Reed Broom, Resin, Roasted Sunflower Seeds Sesame, Soya bean, Spices (excluding Nut Meg, Mace, Cloves, Cassia & Cinnamon), Tobacco, Tomato.
- **18 commodities/items notified by Public Notice No. 106(RE-2008)/2004- 2009 dated 7th November, 2008:** Agarbatti, Bicycle's Spare parts, Blades, Bulbs, Cosmetics, Cotton fabrics, Fertilizers, Imitation jewellery, Insecticides, Leather footwear, Life saving drugs, Menthol, Mosquito

Coils, Paints & Varnishes, Spices, Stainless steel utensils, Sugar & Salt, X Ray paper & Photo paper

- **22 new commodities/items added through this Public Notice No. 30 (RE- 2012)/2009- 2014 dated 16th November, 2012**: Agricultural machinery/equipments/ tools, Bicycle, Bleaching powder, Coal, Edible Oil, Electrical & Electric Appliances, Fabricated steel products, Garments / readymade garments/cloths, Handlooms and handicrafts items, Hardware/minor construction materials and electrical fittings, Lime, Medicines, Milk powder, tea, edible oil, beverages, Motor Cycles & Motor Cycle Spare Parts, Other items such as electronic/musical instruments, stationary item, torch light, Plastic items: water tank, buckets, chairs, plastic pipes and briefcase, Rice, Wheat, Maize, Millets & Oats, Scented tobacco, Semi precious stone, Sewing machines, Textile fabrics, Three wheelers/cars below 1000 CC.

Drivers of India's Policy for Engagement in Myanmar

Essentially, four key considerations have been instrumental in the drafting of India's Myanmar policy in the 1990s. Each of these drivers has been so vital to India's national interest that they have forced it to overlook the concerns of pro-democracy groups in that country.

Presence of China in Myanmar

A former Indian ambassador, Rajiv Bhatia, argues: "Over the years, New Delhi has faced two kinds of criticism on its Myanmar policy. Realists argued that its pro-democracy stance had driven Myanmar into 'China's lap.' Later, they maintained that the engagement was moving too slowly." Authors like Renaud Egreteau argue that India's rapprochement with Myanmar has to be understood in the light of India's worry of being encircled by China." The fact that the dragon had filled the diplomatic vacume by intensifying its relationship with Myanmar since the late 1980s was not lost on India.

India constantly fears that the Chinese influence in Myanmar is spreading day-by-day. Although the Chinese government has always denied of having any military ambitions in Myanmar, American and Indian agencies have constantly claimed that the Chinese are building monitoring facilities at Myanmar's ports in the Bay of Bengal as part of their so-called 'string of pearls' strategy to encircle India. In 1949, Myanmar was one of the first countries to recognise the People's Republic of China. But relations between both countries fluctuated in the 1960s following anti-Chinese riots in Rangoon. The military regime under Gen Ne Win had maintained a policy of equidistance from both India and China though Myanmar's bureaucracy has always been suspicious of its two big neighbours. But after 1988, when the Western countries imposed broad sanctions on Myanmar, and India supported pro-democracy workers, China filled the vacuum, providing aid and weapons and ramping up trade. Northern states in Myanmar were opened up to Chinese trade by the mid-1990s. In mining sector alone, China invested more than $ 1 billion in Myanmar and soon became its fourth largest foreign investor. As per data of World bank bilateral trade between Myanmar and China has reached about about $ 4.73 billion in 2016 which is almost 40% of its total trade As per a recent report appearing in Myanmar daily Mizzima the trade in 2017 has crossed 6.3 billion in 2017. Other than trade Chinese firms are heavily involved in timber logging in Myanmar. Myanmar gives China access to the Indian Ocean, not only for imports of oil and gas and exports from landlocked south-western Chinese provinces, but also for potential military bases.

In addition, Myanmar has been a major recipient of Chinese economic assistance over the past decade generally provided in the form of grants, interest-free loans, concessional loans or debt relief. According to the International Crisis Group, "Chinese economic assistance and cooperation projects are usually given to Chinese state-owned enterprises and are therefore often indistinguishable from state commercial investments. This makes it difficult to account for the complete extent of China's assistance and investments in Myanmar. The official figures also do not give a full indication of the economic relationship between the two countries. Chinese investments are grossly underestimated by Myanmar's official figures and, to a lesser extent, Chinese figures."

The much-hyped multi-billion dollar oil and gas pipeline between Myanmar and China connecting Shwe gas fields in the Irrawaddy delta to China's Yunnan province was formally inaugurated on 29 July 2013 at Mandalay. This project which was inked in 2007 consists of two separate pipelines for crude oil and natural gas: the 793-kilometre gas pipeline and the 771-kilometre oil pipeline. This 793-kilometre pipeline starts from Kuaykphyu in Myanmar and passes through Rakhine state, Magway and Mandalay regions into the Shan State and enters China at Ruili in Yunnan province. En route, the pipeline has six pumping stations. The cost of this gas pipeline has been estimated at USD 2.01 billion. The gas pipeline has a pumping capacity of 12 billion cubic metres and that of the oil pipeline is 22 million tonnes of crude oil per year. Just by allowing the transit, Myanmar is going to get multifarious benefits. The annual transmission of 22 million tons of crude oil through the oil pipeline will bring $ 22 million as well as well as $ 13.6 million in transit fees. Exporting 12 billion cubic metres of gas will bring in $ 1.5 billion. This means a lot for the struggling economy of a nation. Myanmar also gets the rights to use 2 billion cubic metres of natural gas for its domestic use. This is likely to be used by major cities along the pipeline to supply energy to the inland regions, boosting its economy. Over the next 30 years, Myanmar is set to earn a whopping $ 30 billion from this project. This project will create a huge amount of job opportunities for the local people residing around it, hiring as many as over 6,000 for construction work followed others for maintenance work.

The huge investment by China in the pipeline project is understandable to the world. Energy-starved China is looking at hedging its energy-related risks for which it is ready to make any concession. China is also selling a large quantity of arms to Myanmar. When Myanmar opposition parties raised questions about the arms, Chinese officials replied that China only provides major military equipment, not small arms ("the heavy weapons that cannot kill your people"). In recent times, the Myanmar army and navy have been given M-11 rocket components, artillery guns, communication equipment, electric lighting, signal equipment and speedboats by

China. In fact, the Myanmar navy almost resembles PLAN in many ways. China is helping the Myanmar Air Force too for upgradation of its communication equipment and training on the new edition of aviation and border maps. It is also assisting in undertaking a maritime survey of its territory. In August 2010, two Chinese warships docked at Myanmar's Yangon port on a friendly visit, making it the first such visit since 1988. A Chinese diplomat said, "These two navy destroyers arrived at Yangon's Thilawa port on Sunday to promote relations between the two militaries." Additionally, China has acted for a number of years as a protective shield for Myanmar in the United Nations Security Council by vetoing resolutions against the military *junta*. In September 2009, China blocked the inclusion of Myanmar on the agenda of the UN Security Council.

Availability of Energy in Abundance

India is the world's sixth largest energy consumer, accounting for about 3.3 per cent of the world's total annual energy consumption. Despite its large annual energy production, it overall remains an energy importer, basically due to the large imbalance between energy production and consumption. Myanmar's oil and gas reserves are of interest to India because if its future energy requirement. Myanmar has oil reserves of around 600 million barrels and an approximate gas reserve of 88 trillion cubic feet (TCF). Indian companies like the overseas arm of India's Oil and Natural Gas Commission—ONGC Videsh Ltd.(OVL), Gas Authority of India Limited (GAIL) and ESSAR have made investments in the oil and energy sector of Myanmar. It was during the 2001 visit of the then external affairs minister Jaswant Singh to Myanmar that India started seriously thinking about bringing gas from Myanmar. The February 2003 visit of Myanmar's General U Win Aung to India further boosted this cooperation in the hydrocarbon, power and energy sectors, particularly in the exploration of Myanmar's onshore oil and gas reserves. However, in spite of the involvement of OVL and GAIL in exploration activities in the offshore natural gas fields along the Rakhine coast, India has suffered a number of setbacks in getting gas from Myanmar. In 2008, Myanmar withdrew India's status as preferential buyer and started selling gas to China's

National Petroleum Corporation (CNPC) for 30 years from 2013 onwards. Starting October 2009, China started building a crude oil port in Myanmar to cut out the long loop of the Malacca strait. In 2005, Myanmar had declined gas supply to the Myanmar-Bangladesh-India pipeline. Instead, it signed an agreement with Hong Kong-listed Petrochina to which Myanmar agreed to sell 6.5 TCF from A-1 block in Rakhine state through an overland pipeline to Kunming for 30 years. This had made the proposed tri-nation Myanmar-Bangladesh-India pipeline project redundant. However, India has no option but to stay engaged in Myanmar.

Keeping North Eastern Insurgency in Check

For decades, India's north-eastern region has witnessed the growth of insurgency groups with demands ranging from independence, autonomy, tribal rights, etc. There are a large number of such groups and though a number of them have stopped activities, many still continue which continuously hampers the security situation in the region. They have constantly challenged and damaged projects in this region and have impeded the processes of development. The remoteness of the north-eastern region and years of neglect have led to a feeling of alienation in the people of this region. This constantly gives a fillip to these armed movements. In the last two decades, the policy of the Indian government has gone through a process of total transformation and focus on development has commenced. Huge amounts have been made available for the region. However, insurgency groups continue to act as spoilers, trying to resist the developmental process and continue the alienation. Myanmar is contiguous to Mizoram, Nagaland and Manipur, and has helped these armed groups in a variety of ways. Because of the ethnic ties and tribal linkages between the people on either side of border, it has facilitated their movement and given safe haven and camps in those areas. Essays on the insurgency movements give detailed accounts of such activities.

There also have been instances when groups like the PLA of Manipur had their cadres trained in China. In the 1960s a batch from the 'Naga Army' reached China for training travelling through Myanmar and till 1980, China had trained several batches of Naga and Mizo rebels and a few dozen Manipuri rebel leaders. Though it is believed that official Chinese support to these rebels has ended China continues to be a route for procurement of weapons on payment. Many armed groups established their camps in Myanmar in the mid-1970s. This served three purposes: one, safe shelter after East Pakistan collapsed; two, a crucial link through which rebels could move to China for training; and, three, weapons procurement. Much of the purposes still remain valid, even while changes have occurred in the nature and kind of support these groups generate in foreign locations.

At the insistence of India, Myanmar conducted on and off military operations against the north-eastern rebels since the 1980s. India still believes that currently there are some camps of Northeast-based insurgent groups in Myanmar. The long presence of the insurgents in Myanmar has provided them with a vital sense of security. In the event of any long-term military operation in states like Manipur, the insurgents have the option of moving to their bases in Myanmar.

As the counter-insurgency operations by the Indian army have intensified in Manipur, these bases have served as training centres for fresh recruits. Moreover, it is in these camps that the insurgents amass weapons procured from a variety of sources in Southeast Asia and possibly China. Of late, reports indicating a tactical level of understanding between the insurgents and the lower rung cadres of Myanmar's military have emerged. These reports, based on intelligence inputs, point to the bonhomie between the insurgents and the military personnel, largely sustained by regular gifts and money.

In return, the insurgents are warned about impending operations by the forces, thereby allowing them to vacate camps long before the men in uniform arrive. They are also assisted to get contract jobs and carry out their business activities. Reports also indicate that the Myanmar army is using the services of insurgents to keep track and also carry out occasional attacks on Myanmarese rebels, some of whom have formed safe bases on the Indian side. Southeast Asia has long served as a lucrative arms market for north-eastern insurgents. Arms into the northeast have either come through Myanmar or through Bangladesh.

Insurgent camps in Myanmar allow these rebels to stock weapons and slowly transfer them to various places in India. In addition, the north-eastern insurgents have also indulged in smuggling of drugs from Myanmar. The easy availability of drugs has made the youth of states like Manipur, Mizoram and Nagaland vulnerable. This has been articulated to the Indian authorities and New Delhi has consequently initiated measures to enhance the counter-terrorism capacities of the Myanmar army, just not in terms of equipping them with sophisticated weapons and other communication devices but also improving infrastructure along the border areas. In order to secure Myanmar's cooperation and strengthen its control over territories where the north-eastern rebels are camping, India has supplied military hardware to that country.

On 21 May 2010, responding to Myanmar's demands for building new roads along the border areas, the Indian Army handed over heavy machinery and other necessary equipment to its Myanmar counterparts at Moreh. India hopes that the building of roads and other construction in remote and inaccessible areas would improve the overall control of the army over these areas. On 5-6 May 2010 a joint Indo-Myanmar medical, dental and veterinary camp was conducted jointly along the Indo-Myanmar border. Approximately 2,000 locals from both sides of the border benefited from the services of general physicians, specialist doctors, dentists and veterinary doctors of the Indian Army and Assam Rifles as well as medical staff from Myanmar.

India's Support to Democratic Setup in Myanmar

India, acting as a responsible democracy in Asia, has goaded many countries in the neighbourhood to embrace full democracy. Myanmar is one of them. Ever since attaining independence in 1948, the then Prime Minister Pt. Jawaharlal Nehru had supported in many ways Myanmar's tryst with democracy under U Nu. However, due to weak governance and unlimited hunger for power of the ethnic groups, the democratic setup began to crumble and was taken over by the strong army under Gen Ne Win. He ruled till 1988. Due to collapse of the economy during his rule there was widespread unrest. Elections in 1990 resulted in bringing in an iconic leadership by Aung San Suu Kyi. She won the election; however, the military which had tasted power all these years, refused to hand over power and dissolved the prevalent constitution and ruled by decree. India gave full support to the pro-democratic movement but the military government refused to budge and put Aung San Suu Kyi under house arrest. India continued to support the pro-democracy movement in Myanmar in international forums. The Indian stand was made fairly clear by the then External Affairs Minister, Pranab Mukherjee, in 2006. He said that India cannot "export democracy" to neighbouring countries and that India had to deal with governments "as they exist." The situation has remained unchanged since then.

Soon after the military takeover in Myanmar, India offered support to Suu Kyi. In 1993, it awarded Suu Kyi the Jawaharlal Nehru Award for International Understanding. After the results of the 2015 election, analysts in India welcomed the victory of the National League for Democracy (NLD) led by Myanmar's pro-democracy icon Aung San Suu Kyi who formed the new government. These elections were labelled as the first free nationwide polls in 25 years.

"The formation of a government by the NLD, if it takes place, will be positive for India-Myanmar relations," said Vivek Katju, a former Indian ambassador to Myanmar.

C.U. Bhaskar, an analyst with the Society for Policy Studies think-tank based in New Delhi, agreed: "India has long held that having more democracies in its neighbourhood is more desirable. For India, if the NLD comes to power, it will be a cause for satisfaction because India has been nudging Myanmar in this direction for long," Bhaskar said.

After the formation of the new democratic government in Myanmar, its President, Htin Kyaw, visited India on 29 Aug 2016.

Prime Minister Narendra Modi held extensive talks with him in the first top-level engagement with the new government of Aung San Suu Kyi's National League for Democracy and conveyed India's full support to Myanmar's internal peace process. The two sides inked four MoUs to boost cooperation in areas of connectivity, medicine and renewable energy, besides resolving to deepen ties in a range of other sectors, including agriculture, banking and power.

India and Aung San Suu Kyi

Aung San Suu Kyi was born on 19 June 1945 in Yangon. Her father, Aung San, founded the modern Burmese army and negotiated Burma's independence with the British Empire. In 1947, he was assassinated by his own countrymen. She grew up with her mother, Khin Kyi, and two brothers, Aung San Lin and Aung San Oo, in Yangon. Aung San Lin died at the age of eight years by drowning in a lake on the grounds of the house. Her elder brother migrated to San Diego, California, and became a a United States citizen. Aung San Suu Kyi was educated in Methodist English High School during much of her childhood in Myanmar where she was noted for having a talent for learning languages. She speaks four languages: Burmese, English, French and Japanese. By religion, she is a Theravada Buddhist. Suu Kyi's mother, Khin Kyi, gained prominence as a political figure in the newly-formed Burmese government. She was appointed Burmese ambassador to India and Nepal in 1960 and Aung San Suu Kyi followed her there. She studied in the Convent of Jesus and Mary in New Delhi and graduated from Lady Shri Ram College in New Delhi with a degree in politics in 1964.

She received the Nobel Peace Prize in 1991. She was awarded the Jawaharlal Nehru Peace Prize in 1995. In India on 14 November 2012 to deliver the Jawaharlal Nehru memorial lecture at Vigyan Bhavan in New Delhi, she mentioned that Jawaharlal Nehru and Mahatma Gandhi were the two Indian leaders with whom she felt 'closest' to and recalled how her father, Gen Aung San, was a personal friend of Jawaharlal Nehru. She did not fail to mention the aspects of closeness they shared. After the speech, she visited her alma mater, Lady Sri Ram College.

Aung San Suu Kyi's party, the NLD, after winning the 2015 election formed the government in Myanmar and for the first time in 60 years it was a civilian government. As the new constitution debars her to stand for the office of president, she took upon herself control of the foreign ministry keeping a tight control.

2016 Visit to New Delhi

In Oct 2016 Aung San Suu Kyi concluded a four-day trip to India, signifying a historic visit on her part to maintain cordial relations between the two countries as well as to develop ties with emerging nations at this year's BRICS summit.

This visit comes at a pivotal point in Myanmar's history as the fledgling democracy slowly opens up to the outside world after decades of rule by military generals. Albeit the progress has been slow, yet since the end of Suu Kyi's house arrest in 2010, there has been gradual steps towards opening up to the international community. After the landslide victory in 2015, Aung San Suu Kyi, as the foreign affairs minister, has sought to bolster the bilateral relations with India.

The visit commenced with meeting Indian Prime Minister Narendra Modi. After receiving a bust of Mahatma Gandhi and inspecting a guard of honour, she soon entered talks regarding a number of crucial issues affecting the two countries, including militancy across the Indo-Myanmar border.

However, the bilateral relations have been dominated by the expanding economy of China and the potential implications it may represent for the two nations. The Indian government has had a history of engaging with the military regime of Myanmar for decades, leading to accusations that Suu Kyi may favour the Chinese as a preferential partner. Yet she stated, "We want to keep good terms with all our neighbours." Such engagement can be exemplified through her role at the BRICS-BIMSTEC summit in Goa, leading a delegation at the request of the Indian government, choosing to invite a cluster of nations within the Bay of Bengal Initiative for Multi-Sectoral Technical and Economic Cooperation (BIMSTEC) over its adversary, Pakistan, with whom relations have been strained following a cross-border terror strike in Kashmir.

India can indeed pick and choose its political allies and ties have been further strengthened with Myanmar following Aung San Suu Kyi's visit. Myanmar, as a nation often surrounded in mystery due to the dark curtain during military rule, has much economic potential. It indeed makes a fine choice for Indian engagement in the region.

Peep into the Future of Relations

For many years India's ties with Myanmar were strained as it pledged support for the pro-democratic participants and distanced itself from the military regime. China took advantage this and engaged with the regime as has been brought out in the preceding chapters of this book. In the mid-1990s, then Prime Minister P.V. Narasimha Rao realized that India's aspirations for relations with Southeast Asia would remain a dream without establishing a working relationship with Myanmar.

Over the past two decades, India began to engage with its eastern neighbour slowly but steadily. While in the investment and bilateral trade aspects, India lags far behind China, in terms of assistance it has focused on assisting Myanmar with institution and capacity building which includes English-language training, IT and agriculture.

In 2012, Manmohan Singh became the first Indian prime minister to visit Myanmar in 25 years. He also met the then opposition leader Aung San Suu Kyi. This was followed by the current Prime Minister Narendra Modi's also visit to Myanmar in 2014 when met not only President Thein Sein but also the then the leader of opposition Aung San Suu Kyi. Given her close association with India, political ties with India could strengthen in all areas. In a recent interview, she mentioned her education in India and her links with the Indian relationship.

After the emergence of a full democratic set-up in Myanmar since March 2016, it can now be said with total certitude that India-Myanmar relations are poised to strengthen exponentially. Already there is a notable spurt in bilateral discussions and agreements in just the past few months. The announcements on regional connectivity and trade agreement were made on 17 and 18 February as part of the eighth edition of the India-ASEAN Delhi Dialogue. This included renewed commitment to complete the 3,200-km India-ASEAN trilateral highway that extends from Moreh in India to Mae Sot in Thailand via Mandalay in Myanmar. Nine border *haats* or border trading posts are being considered along the 1,640-kilometre land border with Myanmar.

India's four north-eastern states share borders with Myanmar. India also shares the water boundary of the Bay of Bengal including the strategically important Andaman and Nicobar islands. Myanmar's ports and land corridors provide direct access to the rest of the Asian countries. India, in turn, needs a stable neighbour in the east to control, consolidate and cater better to the northeastern region. It also needs consistent, long-term policies along with diversity in its engagements with Myanmar to ensure better reach in the subcontinent and the greater Indian Ocean region. India's interest in Myanmar in this context can be narrowed down to two factors: one, containing insurgency in the north-east and better integration of these regions; second, a broader engagement which will include institutional and capacity building, economic investments and greater cross-border connections.

In addition there are areas where India, Myanmar and China can actually cooperate. One such is BCIM (Bangladesh, China, India, Myanmar) generally referred to as an important component of China's massive 'One Belt, One Road' project. India has long been sceptical of this project with many analysts believing that it was being used to strengthen China's 'String of Pearls.' Now that there is an increasing interest and regular meetings are being held, India believes that this will help give teeth to its 'Act East' policy. While India and China may compete in some areas, Myanmar's geographical location is such that there is plenty of room for a healthy, cooperative relationship.

In Sep 2017 PM Narender Modi after attending the BRICS summit in China visited Myanmar for two days sending direct signal to the world the importance which India is giving to its eastern neighbour. This was Indian PM's second visit to Myanmar in last three years.

The construed aim of the visit was to strengthen the existing ties and give fillip to the Indian projects in Myanmar.

If one were to look beyond strategic and economic ties, Myanmar could learn from India's very stable democracy. For this, strong institutions are essential, as is religious harmony. Myanmar has a number of choices to make. It can choose to follow the trajectory of Thailand or it can model itself on India which enjoys a stable democracy. For this, Myanmar also needs to ensure that all religions receive equal rights; in this context, the rights of the minority Rohingya need to be safeguarded. A weak democracy and religious intolerance are a lethal cocktail—Pakistan is evidence of this. For its part, India needs to be supportive, while avoiding any suggestion that it is being obtrusive or patronizing.

6

IMPACT OF CHINA–MYANMAR STRATEGIC TIES ON INDIA–MYANMAR RELATIONS

Introduction

Over a period of time, the regime in Myanmar has realised that it has a special place between the two Asian giants, India and China and that both are equally important for its sustenance. It has a 2,200–kilometre border with China and a 1,600-kilometre border with India and is used to seeking help from both while maintaining its independence. During the military regime of the last 20 years, China and Myanmar developed strong strategic bonds and Myanmar almost became an 'economic colony' of China due to its over-dependence for obtaining military hardware, military training, infrastructure development projects and support in international forums. This was a clear result of widespread sanctions imposed on Myanmar by the USA, UK and other European countries after the military regime refused to transfer the power of governance to the elected members after the 1990 general election. In this election, the National League of Democracy (NLD) had won a clear majority under the leadership of Aung San Suu Kyi. The military *junta* not only rejected the verdict of the people but also imprisoned the elected representatives, i.e., the elected members of parliament. This action was viewed very seriously by the UN and other Western nations. They immediately imposed economic and trade sanctions against it. During this period, India supported the pro-democracy leadership under Aung San Suu Kyi and shunned the regime of the military *junta*. Myanmar was almost isolated. The vacuum thus created was filled by China who defied the West and offered to help Myanmar in all aspects.

The deepening of ties on trade, military and infrastructure development became the saving hallmark of the weak economy of Myanmar. The immediate supply of military hardware gave the military regime of Myanmar a shot in the arm as it was finding it difficult to control the ebullient ethnic insurgent groups which were all armed and constantly waging war against the regime, seeking freedom as was promised in the Panglong conference of 1947. After being equipped with the latest weaponry, the military regime was able to control or rather suppress them effectively. Further, in 2007, China thwarted the UN resolution against Myanmar which was mooted by the USA and supported by other European nations. The world was surprised at this development of China openly supporting the military regime of Myanmar known for its human rights violations and when it grabbed the coveted oil and gas pipeline contract in 2008 to pump gas from Shwe oil fields into Kunming the motive became clear to all. Recently, in 2016, the defence ministers of both China and Myanmar pledged to further boost military ties. This was reported by *Xinhua*, the Chinese news agency.

On the Indian front, India had opened its dialogue and engagement with the military *junta* by the mid-1990s as part of its 'Look East Policy' initiative by the Narasimha Rao government. China, by then, had made deep forays in investment reaching almost USD 16 billion dollars. India also pushed in its investment and opened new avenues of border trade with Myanmar from the four eastern states which share borders with Myanmar.

Imperatives of China-Myanmar Strategic Ties

Over the years, China has made considerable effort to improve relations with its neighbours with the goal of maintaining peaceful borders and a viable trading environment. In so doing, it has undertaken significant diplomatic efforts for maintaining cordial relations with governments and governing elites. As time passes, one of the main shortcomings of this policy is becoming exceedingly evident: China is increasingly finding itself at loggerheads with non-governmental actors. Officially, China has in the past described its interests in Myanmar for maintaining stability, border security, security of its huge investments, and connecting land-locked Yunnan to lucrative markets. In pursuing these interests, however, it has become difficult for China to cover the prevalent negative image all across Myanmar.

The following are seen as emerging imperatives from China-Myanmar Strategic Ties of the last two-and-a-half decades:

(a) **Creating land bridge to the Indian Ocean**. It is well known that the only sea face open to China is towards the east and it is completely landlocked from the south. Secondly, the southern province of Yunnan has been seeing slow growth for a long time. Unable to woo Nepal and Bangladesh, it began its forays into Myanmar which fructified reasonably in the last two decades. China's state-run corporation bagged the oil and gas pipeline contract from Shwe gas field and gas and oil will is being pumped via a total of 1,100 kilometre of two pipelines into Kunming, capital of Yunnan. China's outlet to the Indian Ocean is also with an aim for improving naval cooperation in future.

(b) **Supply of military hardware**: This was carried out by China on the behest of Myanmar in the 1990s when the military regime there was grossly lacking military weaponry.

(c) **Controlling ethnic insurgency in border areas**: The strategic ties of the above-mentioned countries were also influenced by the large number of ethnic groups which were staying in the border areas. All these groups were armed and waging minor wars against the Myanmar forces. China wanted to restore stability of the border areas.

(d) **Energy requirements of Yunnan**: Yunnan is an energy-lacking state of China and therefore remained considerably underdeveloped for a long time. Industries in Yunnan needed not only new markets but also energy to run them.

(e) **Establishing 'String of Pearls' around India**: China is well known to be befriend all the small nations around the periphery of India. Myanmar with 1,640 kilometres of borders with India is thus a very lucrative opportunity to contain India.

(f) **ASEAN Link**: China's strategic interest also comprises Myanmar's support for China at the 'ASEAN Plus Three' meet and Greater Mekong sub-regional economic cooperation. Although China gained an advantage in Myanmar due to the latter's international isolation in the past, currently Myanmar is grabbing the viable alternatives to balance China. China can no longer take Myanmar for granted as its unconditional ally in order to enhance its regional strategic agenda.

Effect of Political Reforms on Myanmar-China Relations

After the 2011 election and return of Aung San Suu Kyi to the parliament of Myanmar, the erstwhile pariah nation embarked on a new path of political reforms. These reforms contributed to visible positive changes internally and externally. Internally, the government under President Thein Sein carried out many reforms like granting amnesty to political prisoners, relaxing press censorship and implementing new labour laws that permitted the setting up of unions. The victory of the NLD (winning 42 out of 45 seats contested) in the by-elections of 2012 was a turning point in Myanmar's history. Besides, the government under Thein Sein reached a ceasefire agreement with the Karen National Union (KNU) that ended a major civil conflict in the country. As a result of such reforms, relations with the USA saw an improvement when US Secretary of State Hillary Clinton paid a visit to Naypidaw in 2011 to encourage further reforms. It was the first such high-level visit in almost 50 years. Myanmar formally joined ASEAN in 2014.

This was followed by the EU lifting many sanctions. It also permitted top Myanmar government officials to travel to EU countries. The Australian government lifted restrictions and encouraged other positive steps.

In 2013, the Japanese finance minister visited Myanmar. In a first move, his country waived a huge debt and resumed economic aid and private investments. Thus political reforms in Myanmar have considerably affected Myanmar-China relations in strategic, economic and political terms.

After the 2010 election and President Thein Sein's blitzkrieg of reforms, there was a sudden decrease in the level of frequency of visits from China probably as it never expected such rapid political reforms.

In economic terms, the suspension of work on the Myitsone dam project shocked China. With repercussions from the Myitsone suspension, the broad resentment against Chinese projects including the CNPC oil and gas pipeline project and the NORICO copper mine project changed Chinese investment behaviour. Moreover, Chinese companies were faced with competition from American, European, Japanese and Korean companies that are seeking into entering the last underdeveloped market in Southeast Asia. Very wisely, the Thein Sein government sacrificed Chinese economic interests to gain the friendship of the West. Now, Chinese companies are facing huge competition from American, European, Japanese and Korean companies. As per Y Sun, China lost the Yangon–Naypyidaw high speed railway contract to Japan because Naypyidaw lost its confidence in Chinese technology after the Wenzhou high-speed train collision in July 2011.

The shift in Myanmar's policy in grabbing viable alternatives to balance China can clearly be seen now. China cannot take Myanmar for granted any more as its unconditional ally of the past. The United States engagement with Myanmar and the sudden improvement of their ties considerably reduced China's strategic influence in Myanmar and the region.

Has China been Unsuccessful in Wooing Myanmar?

The answer to this question is affirmative but with an uncanny catch. China's long-term policy of pursuing relations at the inter-governmental level has sown negative perceptions among various ethnic communities in Myanmar. From controversial investments like Myitsone dam which had serious social and environmental impacts, to single-minded efforts to protect its investments, China is now part and parcel of many of Myanmar's deep-rooted problems. Till three years ago, China had failed to anticipate any significant changes in the previous ruling military *junta's* tactics. President Thein Sein had led the country in a more democratic direction than Beijing ever expected. The fast pace of democratic and press reforms and the impact which it had on its investments and other economic ventures in the country was beyond anybody's comprehension.

In spite of the shift, Beijing maintained relations at bilateral inter-state level to gainfully promote its key strategic interests: stability in border regions and protection of its huge investments in the country. As soon as Thein Sein began implementing various democratizing reforms, including a loosening of restrictions on critical news reporting, China suffered setbacks in both areas.

In the past, China had consistently defended Myanmar in international forums including at the United Nations Security Council while the West punished the military-led government through various economic and financial sanctions. Now, pro-China commentators complain that Myanmar's civilian government has chosen to favour investment and relations with the West, including the United States, over China.

So the moot question still remains unanswered as to what aspect of China's foreign policy towards Myanmar left its interests so badly exposed?

Firstly, Beijing has underestimated its own role and influence in Myanmar while the lack of policy coordination among various state and private actors had sent mixed messages to Naypyidaw. Beijing's long-standing rhetoric of non-interference in the internal affairs of other countries, meanwhile, has outlived its usefulness and obviously does not comply with its historical or contemporary actions. While the West imposed punitive sanctions against the previous military regime, China built considerable influence with Myanmar's ruling generals. Approvals of new Chinese investments rose sharply between 1991 and 2010. The general election in 2010 marked a shift from direct military to quasi-civilian rule—though the armed forces still maintained a strong role in politics. After the 2015 election the scenario for Chinese investments is still not so cordial.

Controversial Practices of Chinese Companies in Myanmar

The dubious business practices of Chinese entrepreneurs have triggered widespread local complaints. In 2015, a court in Myitkyina, the capital of Kachin state, sentenced 153 Chinese nationals to life imprisonment after they were found to be involved in illegal logging, according to the Myanmar government. Severe sentences were handed down to these Chinese loggers arrested in these raids. While Beijing has continuously expressed concern about stability and security in the border regions with Myanmar, it has surprisingly done very little to mitigate them. This is particularly true in Kachin state where armed hostilities between the government and the Kachin Independence Army re-erupted in 2011 after 18 years of a ceasefire agreement.

Despite serious security implications, China has demonstrated a lack of understanding of the circumstances behind the renewed conflict. Chinese companies still prefer to deal with the central government and their affiliated military networks in the previous government rather than engaging with local communities, particularly among ethnic groups situated in resource-rich border areas. The underlying justification has traditionally been that ethnic groups are part of separatist movements that lack formal political recognition.

To date, China has shown little interest in joining wider international efforts to assist the peace process in Kachin state. Meanwhile, key issues in Myanmar's fragile political transition, including reduction of the military's role in politics and the resolution of long-standing conflicts between ethno-nationalist groups are testing China's previous grip on the country. Beijing's response so far has only served to damage rather than protect its substantial interests in Myanmar.

Indian Forays in Engaging with Myanmar

Seeing the forays being made by China in Myanmar, India adopted its famous 'Look East Policy' in the early Nineties. The next few years saw a number of visits by high dignitaries from India and Myanmar. India, whilst still supportive of the pro-democracy movement, began to actively engage with the military *junta* and tried to revive old ties. Shyam Saran, the former Indian ambassador to Myanmar in 1997, said that "the relations were still frigid." In November 2000, Gen Maung Aye, the second-most prominent leader of Myanmar's military *junta*, brought a high-powered delegation including Deputy Prime Minister Lt. Gen. Tin Hla along with a team ministers to New Delhi. The then Indian Home Minister, L.K. Advani, tried to break the frigidity and talked about warming of ties between the two countries. This visit was followed by a six-day visit of Gen Than Shwe to New Delhi in 2004 and in 2006 President Abdul Kalam visited Yangon. During these visits, a number of bilateral treaties were signed relating to sharing of cultural, social, technological and military cooperation. Subsequent years saw the Government of India's active involvement in over a dozen projects in Myanmar, both in infrastructural and non-infrastructural areas. These include upgradation and resurfacing of the 160-kilometre long Tamu-Kalewa-Kalemyo road; construction and upgradation of the Rhi-Tiddim Road in Myanmar and the mega Rs 1,500crore Kaladan Multimodal Transport Project, which is going to link the north-eastern states via the Bay of Bengal and Myanmar route. An ADSL project for a high-speed data link in 32 Myanmar cities has been completed by TCIL. ONGC, GAIL and ESSAR are participants in the energy sector in Myanmar. M/s RITES is involved in development of the rail transportation system and in supply of railway coaches, locomotives and spare parts. In September 2008, NHPC signed an agreement for development of the Samantha and Shwezaye Hydro-Electric Power project in Chindwin River. A heavy turbo-truck assembly plant set up in Myanmar by TATA Motors with Government of India financial assistance was inaugurated on December 31, 2010.

Other projects include revamping of the Ananda temple in Bagan, upgradation of the Yangon children's hospital and Sittwe general hospital. India has also assisted in the reconstruction of a high school and six primary schools in Tarlay township, the area worst affected by the severe earthquake that struck north-eastern Myanmar in March 2011.

However what needs to be kept in mind by Indian industry and the Government is the wider interest of the north-eastern states so that the dividends of growth are seen on both sides of the border. A proper roadmap of government-industry cooperation and development should include sectors that not only give inclusive growth to Myanmar but also regional growth for our north-eastern states. We must think in terms of harnessing the energy reserves in Myanmar and also create some energy-processing hubs in the north-eastern states for subsequent usage in the development of adjoining areas. Setting up of an ancillary industry to supply for specific projects in Myanmar can also be planned and some economic zones can be specified for such a purpose. The proposals must also stress upon the development of road and communication infrastructure to support the projects undertaken through the land route. A proper planning of the projects can have a long-term impact on the development of the economies of both Myanmar and Northeast India. It's time for us to reframe our 'Look-East' Policy to make it into 'Look-East through North-East.' High-level visits have been a regular feature of India-Myanmar relations for several years and it increased after the new government came to power in 2010.

President Thein Sein paid a state visit to India on October 12-15, 2011 and had a meeting with the Prime Minister of India, Dr. Manmohan Singh, which was followed by delegation-level talks. President Thein Sein was accompanied by Chief of General Staff

Lt Gen Hla Htay Win and 11 Union Ministers and one Union Deputy Minister and senior officials. In December 2011, the Speaker of Pyithu Hluttaw (Lower House), Thura U Shwe Mann led a high-level parliamentary delegation to India. The objective of the visit was to share India's experience in parliamentary practices and procedures with the visiting Myanmar delegation. Myanmar Foreign Minister U Wunna Maung Lwin paid an official visit to India from January 22 to 26, 2012. These visits were finally followed by Prime Minister Dr. Manmohan Singh's visit to Myanmar in May 2012. During the visit, several new initiatives were announced and 12 MoUs and agreements were signed including extension of a new line of credit (LOC) worth USD 500 million.

Regional Security Balance

After assuming office in 2014 PM Narender Modi visited Myanmar and carried out interaction with the Thein Sein Government as well as Aung San Suu Kyi. After elections the new government was made by the the Aung San Suu Kyi led political Party NLD in Mar 2016. The visit of the President of the newly elected Government, Htin Kyaw to India in Aug 2016 was seen as a very significant step in India-Myanmar relations. During this visit, PM Modi and President Kyaw had wide-ranging and extensive talks on all facets of bilateral relations which included stability on the border and various measures to expand trade and commerce. Decision was also taken to complete the delayed projects at an early date. Immediately after the meeting of the head of states the PMO tweeted, "President (Kyaw) and I agreed to work together for the safety and security of our people. Our engagement is supporting projects in connectivity, infrastructure, capacity building education, healthcare and many other sectors". In the present milieu it is a great opportunity for India and India Inc to expand into Myanmar and subsequently into the ASEAN region using Myanmar as a land bridge. This will also give India a greater role as a regional player.

There is an urgent need for putting in place unambiguous policies and hasten up the measures for multi-sectarian trade and commerce projects on one hand and strategic partnership with Myanmar on the other hand. With a stable democratic set up in Myanmar and a stable government in India this can be the most conducive time to get into a 'comprehensive strategic partnership' for security of our western borders in the short run and maintaining regional security balance in the long run.

7

Conclusions and Road Ahead

Myanmar is strategically important to India as it is the only ASEAN country that shares a border with India. It is also the only country that can act as a link between India and other ASEAN countries. India and Myanmar also have strong historical links not only with the British colonial era but were linked even before it. Today, Myanmar can be considered India's gateway to Southeast Asia and could give the required impetus to realize India's 'Look East Policy.' India has also decided to upgrade the Kalewa-Yargyi road segment to highway standards, while Myanmar would develop the Yargyi-Monywa portion. This would help to connect Moreh in India to Mae Sot in Thailand via Myanmar. This, in turn, would improve India's connectivity and relationship with both Myanmar and Thailand.

If India is to become an assertive and important regional player in Asia, it has to work towards developing policies that would improve and strengthen it internally which will encourage more confidence in its ability to lead the region and be an important regional player. Competition with China should also be taken seriously. China's growing influence in the region would lead to a more one-sided dynamic in the region. China has asserted itself reasonably well in Asia and Southeast Asia through its trade and economic relations. With Myanmar it has taken up large infrastructure projects in that country. India on the other hand needs to use its soft power more effectively and at the same time strengthen itself domestically and regionally.

There are several advantages that India has over China with regard to Myanmar. One is the democratic process. With the outcome of the 2015 election and restoration of full democracy in Myanmar, India's position stands to gain substantially and China's stands to lose. This was evident in the September 2016 visit of Aung San Suu Kyi in September this year when a Shanghai-based think-tank acknowledged that India had lesser barriers in building its relations with Myanmar than China had, which had very strongly supported its military regime and neglected the pro-democracy agitators. Bordering Myanmar is India's northeastern region which has long suffered from an underdeveloped economy. New Delhi needs to enhance its collaboration with Myanmar in the border areas for economic reasons. Zhao Gancheng, director of the think tank, wrote in an op-ed published in the *Global Times* on September 14, 2016.

According to him, "more importantly, India sees the comprehensive strategic cooperative partnership between Beijing and Myanmar as a threat. It hence feels the urge to take the offensive by cozying up to Myanmar in order to gain more influence in the country as leverage to counterbalance China."

The write-up made a reference to Prime Minister Narendra Modi's meeting with Aung San Suu Kyi on the sidelines of the just-concluded India-Asian summit and the East Asia Summit in Laos in which he assured Suu Kyi that India stands by Myanmar.

There is also respect for institutions that is strong enough to hold the country together. Finally, cooperation in different multilateral forums such as ASEAN and BIMSTEC strengthen the relationship between the two countries. Besides, India has sent a clear signal that while economic ties are important, it is keen to build a holistic relationship and is prepared to assist in institution building in Myanmar.

While the basic foundation for the relationship between India and

Myanmar has been laid by previous governments, the onus is on the present Indian administration to demonstrate that it can take the relationship to a higher level. It can also become a strong regional player through a more proactive approach. Myanmar has pursued a hedging strategy in the face of rising China since 1989. Temporarily, Myanmar has depended on China for the sake of the regime's survival. However, Myanmar has always been cautious about the potential threat of its giant neighbour, China. Myanmar sought to maintain its sovereignty and national security by playing its geo-strategic location and the energy card. Moreover, Myanmar tried to diversify its external relations with India, Russia and ASEAN countries for the sake of attaining alternatives to mitigate its over-dependence on China. Following domestic political reforms since 2011, Myanmar's policy toward China favoured soft balancing underpinned by the rapid improvement of external relations with the USA, the EU countries and Japan. However, Myanmar will not alienate China because it will seek to meet its economic interests and political interests by recalibrating its relations with China, the USA and the other powers in the region. Consequently, Myanmar will move towards not only China but also to any other power in order to enhance its economic and political gains.

It has become increasingly apparent that the bilateral relationship between China and Myanmar is not without its problems. In fact, Naypyidaw is increasingly trying to reduce the Chinese influence in Myanmar. On the Chinese side, there is an apparent benefit in utilizing Myanmar in China's security strategy but there seems to be major problems in accomplishing this, not least related to its own naval weaknesses and complicated relationship with Myanmar. However, both Myanmar and China are dependent on each other for a number of reasons. China is most likely to continue to support Naypyidaw, but also the minority groups in northern Myanmar, even without a change of government. The long-term results will be one of two outcomes. One is that the international community opens up to Myanmar and reduces China's influence which will result in stable political transition over time. This would most likely strengthen Chinese links with the Kokang, Wa and Kachin minority groups but reduce it with Myanmar at large. The other outcome is that the political liberalization suffers a setback with the outside world continuing its old policy of containment and sanctions, which will inevitably strengthen Chinese influence both in the minority regions and in Myanmar at large. The ball is in the international community's court; something that has been realized and yet nothing significant has happened. China's primary interest at present is not to increase its military might in and around Myanmar but rather to secure economic development and, more importantly, regional stability. With this in mind it is clear that in the short to medium term there are no indications that China's limited military cooperation with Myanmar will have a major impact on Southeast Asia or on international interests. The reasons are that China is reluctant to strain its improved relations with other Southeast Asian countries and appear uncooperative on the international stage while Myanmar is reluctant to rely too much on China since the benefits are minimal for the moment and there are ample opportunities to increase cooperation with new actors. What could change this and increase the Chinese influence is an international boycott of Myanmar that forces Naypyidaw to rely on China for economic and political support. It is apparent that China does not have the military capacity or willingness to expand too far beyond its national borders. Its focus is to take 'one pearl' at a time and cooperate with the countries in Southeast Asia. Isolation of Myanmar and, in a worst-case scenario, even China, would be the most likely reason for the establishment of a policy that would be perceived as negative towards China's neighbours and the USA. In the long term, China has a strategic interest in strengthening military cooperation with Myanmar and Southeast Asia at large, including more permanent bases. These interests will impact on the security situation of the Southeast Asian countries, India and the USA. This is not to say that China will have an offensive strategy but, for economic and security reasons, it is logical for China to increase its influence, something that became very apparent during the crisis in Libya. It is beyond doubt that China will increasingly clash with other actors over security concerns in both mainland and maritime Southeast Asia.

The new Indian government has begun its tenure with a busy calendar of international travel. Most recently, External Affairs Minister Sushma Swaraj has been in Naypyitaw, Myanmar, for the ASEAN Foreign Ministers Meeting (AMM), the East Asia Summit meeting of foreign ministers and the ASEAN Regional Forum.

In fact, India and Myanmar have traditionally had much in common with cultural, historical, ethnic and religious ties in addition to sharing a long geographical land border and maritime boundary in the Bay of Bengal. India and Myanmar's relationship officially got underway after the Treaty of Friendship was signed in 1951 after which the foundation for a more meaningful relationship was established during Prime Minister Rajiv Gandhi's visit in 1987. Bilateral ties received another significant boost when the two countries signed a trade agreement in 1994. For many years, India did not open up to the authoritarian regime and it was only over a period of time that India started engaging with the military *junta* of Myanmar.

While the region's focus has revolved around the South Asian Association for Regional Cooperation (SAARC) countries and China, Myanmar is becoming increasingly important for India in both a strategic and economic context. High-level visits have become a regular feature between them. During Prime Minister Manmohan Singh's state visit in 2012, many new initiatives were announced and around a dozen MOUs were signed along with a line of credit for $ 500 million. Many Indian companies made significant economic and trade agreements in infrastructure and other areas. Some of the major projects taken up by India include the resurfacing and upgrading of the 160-kilometre Tamu-Kalewa-Kalemyo road and the Kaladan project that will connect Kolkata Port with Sittwe Port in Myanmar (which is still in progress). A bus service from Imphal to Mandalay will begin in October.

India is also helping Myanmar by setting up high-speed data links in 32 cities. Some other Indian companies such as Essar, GAIL and ONGC Videsh Ltd. have invested in Myanmar's energy sector. Tata Motors has set up a heavy turbo-truck assembly plant with financial assistance from the Indian Government.

Bilateral trade has grown from $ 12.4 million in 1980-1981 to $ 2.52 billion in 2015-2016. Agricultural items like beans and pulses and forest-based products make up nearly 90 percent of India's imports. Myanmar is also the beneficiary of a duty-free tariff preference scheme for least developed countries (LDCs). Both countries also signed a border trade agreement in 1994 and have two trade points along their 1,643-kilometre border. India has also promoted some trade events such as the India Product Show 2012 which represented 19 Indian companies and the NEFIT car rally from Guwahati to Yangon and back, which had 60 participants and was also part of trade promotion. The two countries have shared cultural exchanges through various cultural troupes. One such exchange was in 2009 when Myanmar sent a 13-member student group that attended a SAARC cultural festival in India.

Some Chinese think tanks feel that Myanmar would maintain its independence and tilt neither towards India nor China but maintain its neutrality. However, having completed my research I feel India has a much bigger edge over China as of now with full democracy restored in Myanmar and India should make much bigger forays in terms of engaging with the Aung San Suu Kyi Government which has always been so amenable to India. Now is the time to be a little assertive and establish itself as a strong regional player.

ANNEXURE I

AGREEMENT BETWEEN THE GOVERNMENT OF THE REPUBLIC OF INDIA AND THE GOVERNMENT OF THE UNION OF MYANMAR ON BORDER TRADE BETWEEN THE TWO COUNTRIES

The Government of the Republic of India and the government of the union of Myanmar, being desirous of promoting trade relations between India and Myanmar, and through friendly consultations, have agreed to the formal establishment of border trade on the basis of equality and mutual benefit and have reached the following agreement.

ARTICLE I

The border trade shall be conducted through the following designated customs posts and in accordance with the laws, regulations and procedures in force in either country:

(a) Moreh in India and Tamu in Myanmar
(b) Champai in India and Hri in Myanmar
(c) Other places that may be notified by mutual agreement between the two countries.

Adequate provisions will be made to enable buyers of either country to inspect and take delivery of good at the customs posts in the country of the seller.

The goods to be traded on the border under this agreement shall be as permitted by both governments.

ARTICLE II

Exchange of locally produced commodities as indicated in annexure I, by people living along both sides of the Indo- Myanmar Border will continue as per the prevailing customary practice including the barter mechanism.

ARTICLE III

Trade under the Agreement may be conducted in freely convertible currencies or in currencies mutually agreed upon by the two countries including through counter trade agreements.

ARTICLE IV

This agreement shell be reviewed periodically by both sides to ensure a successful implementation of its objectives and provisions. In case of differences relating to and arising out of this Agreement, the same shall be amicable settled in the spirit of mutual cooperation and friendship.

ARTICLE V

Amendment(s) and/ or supplement(s) to this Agreement shall be made by Exchange of Letter between the two sides.

ARTICLE VI

The Agreement shall come into force with effect from a date mutually agreed upon by the two sides and shall remain in force for two years form that date. It shall be automatically extended for a period of two years at a time unless either side gives notice in writing of its intention to terminated this agreement three months in advance of the date of expiry.

Done in New Delhi on the 21st day of January, 1994 on three originals, in the Hindi, Myanmar and English Languages. The three texts shall be equally authentic, but in case of any divergence of interpretation, the English text shall prevail.

On behalf of the
Government of the
Republic of India

Sd/-
(TEJENDRA KHANNA)
SECRETRY
MINISTRY OF COMMERCE
MINISTRY OF TRADE

On behalf of the
Government of the
Union of Myanmar

Sd/-
(LT. COLONEL KYAW MYINT)
DIRECTOR GENERAL
DIRECTOR OF TRADE

ANNEXURE II

COMMODITIES IDENTIFIED FOR EXCHANGE BY RESIDENTS LIVING ALONG THE BORDER BETWEEN INDIA AND MYANMAR

1. Mustard/ Rape Seed
2. Pulse and beans
3. fresh vegetables
4. Fruits
5. Garlic
6. Onion
7. Chilies
8. Spices (Excluding Nut Meg, Mace, Cassia and Cloves)
9. Bamboo
10. Minor forest products excluding teak
11. Betel nuts and leaves
12. Food items for local consumption
13. Any other commodities as may be mutually agreed.

ADDITIONAL COMMODITIES APPROVED

1. Tobacco
2. Tomato
3. Reed Broom
4. Sesame
5. Resin
6. Coriander Seeds
7. Soyabean
8. Roasted Sunflower Seeds
9. Katha
10. Ginger

List of items permitted for imports under the Border Trade Agreement with Myanmar as on 1 April 2007

Description of goods

1. Rice
2. Pulses and Beans
3. Chana
4. Mustard and Rape seed
5. Ground Nut
6. Fresh Vegetables and Fruits
7. Garlic and Onion
8. Reed Broom
9. Sesame Seeds
10. Betel- Nuts
11. Turmeric
12. Dried Ginger
13. Coriander
14. Dried Chilly (including in powder form)
15. Wood in the rough, whether or not stripped of bark, timber, wood roughly squared, wood swan or chipped lengthwise, sliced of a thickness exceeding 25mm.
16. Bamboo
17. Tomato
18. Sunflower Seeds
19. Resin
20. Catechu
21. Betal Leaves

ANNEXXURE III

To be published in the Gazette of India Extraordinary
(Part I, Section- 1)
Government of India
Minister of Commerce & Industry
Department of Commerce
Directorate General of Foreign Trade
Udyag Bhawan, New Delhi-110011

PUBLIC NOTICE NO. 30 (RE-2012)/2009-2014

NEW DELHI, DATED THE 16TH NOVEMBER, 2012

Subject: Indo-Myanmar Border Trade

1. In exercise of powers conferred under paragraph 2.4 of the Foreign Trade Policy, 2009-14 and in supersession of Public Notice No. 289(PN)/ 92-97 dated 10th April, 1995 and Public Notice No. 106 (RE-2008)/ 2004-2009 dated 7th November, 2008, the Director General of Foreign Trade hereby makes the following arrangements with a view to promote Indo-Myanmar Border Trade:

2. In terms of the provisions contained in the Foreign Trade Policy, import/ export of the following commodities/ items is permitted by the people living along both sides of the Indo Myanmar Border as per the prevailing customary practice:

   I.22 Commodities/items notified by Public Notice No. 289 (PN)/ 92-97 dated 10th April, 1995:

   1. Bamboo, 2 Betal Nuts and Leaves, Chillies, 4. Coriander Seeds, 5. Food Items for Local Consumption, 6. Fresh Vegetables, 7. Fruits, 8. Garlic, 9. Ginger, 10. Katha, 11. Minor forest product (Excluding teak), 12. Mustard/ Rape Seed, 13. Onion, 14. Pulses and Beans, 15. Reed Broom, 16. Resin, 17. Roasted Sunflower Seeds 18. Sesame, 19. Soyabean, 20. Spices (excluding Nut Meg, Mace, Cloves, Cassia & Cinnamon), 21. Tabacco, 22. Tomato.

II.18 Commodities/items notified by Public Notice No. 106 (RE-2008)/ 2004-2009 dated 7th November, 2008:

2. Agarbatti, 2 Bicycle's Spare parts, 3. Blades 4. Bulbes, 5. Cosmetics 6. Cotton fabrics, 7. Fertilizers

8. limitation jewellery, 9. Insecticides,10. Leather footwear, 11. Life saving drugs,12. Menthol, 13. Mosquito Coils,14. Paints & Varnishes, 15. Spices, 16. Stainless steel utensils, 17. Sugar & Salt 18. X Ray paper & Photo paper.

III.22 new Commodities/ items added through this Public Notice:

1. Agriculture machinery/ equipment/ tools, 2. Bicycle, 3. Bleaching powder, 4. Coal, 5. Edible Oil, 6. Electrical & Electric Appliances, 7. Fabricated steel products, 8. Garments / readymade garments/ cloths, 9. Handlooms and handicrafts items, 10. Hardware/ minor construction materials and electrical fittings, 11. Lime 12. Medicines, 13, Milk powder, tea edible oil, beverages, 14. Motor Cycles & Motor Cycle Spare Parts, 15. Other items such as electronic/musical instruments, stationary item, torch light, 16.plastic items: water tank, buckets, chairs, Plastic pipes and briefcase, 17. Rice, Wheat, Maize & Oats, 18. Scented tobacco, 19. Semi precious stone, 20. Sewing machines, 21. Textile fabrics, 22. Three wheelers/ cars below 100 CC.

3. **Effect of Public Notice**

i Existing arrangement for import/ export of commodities/ items under Indo Myanmar Border have been revised; and

ii 22 new commodities/ items have been added to the existing list of 40 tradable items and all the 62 commodities/ items consolidated.

Sd/-

(Anup K. Pujari)

Director General of Forein Trade

E- mail: dgft@nic.in

(issued from F.No. 01/89/180/Misc. 49/AM-04/PC-I (A). Vol. III)

RESERVE BANK OF INDIA
Mumbai- 400 001

RBI/2015-16/230 **November 05, 2015**
A. P. (DIR Series) Circular No. 26

To

All Authorised Dealers in Foreign Exchange

Madam / Sir,

Switching from Barter Trade to Normal Trade at the Indo-Myanmar Border

1. Attention of the Authorised Dealers is invited to A.D. (G.P. Series) Circular No.8 dated May 17, 1997 read with A.P.(DIR Series) Circular No. 17 dated October 16, 2000 in terms of which it has been stipulated that the border trade between Myanmar and India may be settled through barter system. Further, in terms of Regulation 3 and 5 of the Notification No. FEMA 14/ 2000-RB dated May 3, 2000 [viz. Foreign Exchange Management (Manner of Receipt and Payment) Regulations, 2000] as amended from time to time, the trade transactions with Myanmar may be settled in any permitted currency in addition to the Asian Clearing Union mechanism.

2. Barter trade was initially permitted to facilitate exchange of locally produced commodities along the Indo-Myanmar border. As such, these transactions were not captured in the banking system or reflected in the trade statistics. However, over a period of time the trade basket has diversified and adequate banking presence is in place to support normal trade with Myanmar.

3. It has, therefore, been decided, in consultation with Government of India, to do away with the barter system of trade at the Indo-Myanmar border and switch over completely to normal trade with effect from December 1, 2015. Hence instructions contained in A.P. (DIR Series) Circular No. 17 dated October 16, 2000, stand withdrawn. Accordingly, all trade transactions with Myanmar, including those at the Indo-Myanmar border with effect from

December 1, 2015 would be settled in any permitted currency in addition to the Asian Clearing Union mechanism.

4. Authorised Dealers may bring the contents of this circular to the notice of their constituents concerned.

5. Reserve Bank has also amended the Principal Regulations through the Foreign Exchange Management (Export of Goods & Services) (Second Amendment) Regulations, 2015 notified through Notification No FEMA.347/2015-RB dated July 24, 2015, vide G.S.R. No 579 (E) dated July 24, 2015.

4. The directions contained in this circular have been issued under Section 10(4) and Section 11(1) of the FEMA, 1999 (42 of 1999) and are without prejudice to permissions / approvals, if any, required under any other law.

Yours faithfully,

(A. K. Pandey)
Chief General Manager

BIBLIOGRAPHY

Primary Sources

ASEM. 2009. "9th Asia-Foreign Ministers Meeting Chair Statement." Hanoi, Vietnam, 26 May.

Asia Yearbook 1994, pp. 98-100; Peter W. Rodman, 'China Woos Burma,' *International Herald Tribune*, 30 May 1997, http://www.mmtimes.com/2012/news/618/news61814.html.

'A New Chapter in US- Burma Relations,' VOA editorial, 23 May 2012.

Asia Times, http://www.atimes.com/atimes/Southeast_Asia/SEA-01-180313.html

BBC (2012), 'U.S. to Exchange Ambassadors with Burma,' 13 January, online: www.bbc.co.uk/news/world-asia-16554415 (13 January 2012).

BBC, November 19, 2012. http://www.bbc.co.uk/news/world-asia-20386066

China Seeks to Regain Role in Changed Myanmar: Experts,' *South China Morning Post*, 5 Apr 2013.

'China's Myanmar Dilemma,' International Crisis Group, Asia Report No.177, 14 September 2009, http:// www.crisisgroup.org/en/regions/asia/north-east-asia/china/177-chinas-myanmar-dilemma.aspx

'China Oil Pipelines,' http://en.wikipedia.org/wiki/Kazakhstan%E2%80%93China_oil_pipeline.

'China Oil Demand,' July 15, 2013, *Reuters*, http://www.reuters.com/article/2013/07/15/china-oil-demand idUSL4N0FL0Q320130715.

'Chinese Warships Pay Visit to Myanmar,' 30 August 2010, http://

www.earthtimes.org/articles/news/341623,pay-visit myanmar.html.

'China Pledges Support for New Myanmar Government,' *Myanmar Times*, 6 April.

'China to Improve Military Ties with Myanmar, Says Senior Official, *MIZZIMA*, 10 Sep 2016, http://www.mizzima.com/news-domestic/china-improve-military-ties-myanmar-says-senior-official

'China, Myanmar to Further Increase Military Cooperation, *MIZZIMA*, 26 May 2016, http://www.mizzima.com/news-regional/china-myanmar-further-increase-military-cooperation

Development, *F. India*, 19 Oct 2016, http://www.firstpost.com/india/narendra-modi-meets-aung-san-suu-kyi-hold-talks-on-border-security-and-development-3059936.html

'Democratic Myanmar Moves to Deepen its Ties with ASEAN,' *World Politics Review* (WPR),13 Jul 2016, http://www.worldpolitics review.com/trendlines/19355/democratic-myanmar-moves-to-deepen-its-ties-with-asean

'Dynamics of the Complex China-Myanmar-India Triangle to Soon become Clearer,' *Hindustan Times*, 22 Aug, 2016 http://www.hindustantimes.com/analysis/dynamics-of-the complex-china-myanmar india—triangle-to-soon-become clearer/story-jS74j5ALIQ65kRaP8O80iP.html

'Enhancing India-Myanmar Trade and investment Relations: A brief analysis,' Export - 'Myanmar Beckons,' *The Times of India*, May 29, 2012.

'Factbox: Pipelines From Myanmar to China,' *Reuters*, http://www.reuters.com/article/idUSTRE6120MQ2 0100203. Accessed on 29 April 2010.

'Five Facts about China-Myanmar Relations,' *Reuters*, 1 June 2010, http://in.reuters.com/article/ idINIndia-48959920100601.

Indo-Myanmar Relations, Ministry of External Affairs, Government of India, http://mea.gov.in/mystart. php?id=5004450.2.

India Myanmar Expanding Bilateral Cooperation, CII note 2013.

Indo-Myanmar Border Trade, DGFT Public Notice No.30/(RE 2012)/2009-14.

India Myanmar Set Trade target of $ 3bn by 2015,' Press Trust of India, 07 Jun 2013.

'India, Myanmar and Thailand Discuss Trilateral Connectivity,' Press Trust of India, 11 Sep 2012.

'Indo Myanmar Mega Medical and Fraternisation Dental & Vet. Camp,' *Imphal Free Press*, 7 May 2010.

'India Promises Whole-hearted Support to Myanmar,' PTI, 29 Aug 2016, http://www.deccanherald.com/content/567530/india-promises-whole-hearted-support.html

'India looks to improve defence ties with Myanmar,' *Deccan Herald*, 25 July 2015.

International Crisis Group, China's Myanmar Dilemma, 17.19.20.

'Intolerent Myanmar,' *Bangkok Posts Opinion*, 5 Sep 2012.

'India threatened by China-Myanmar ties: Chinese think-tank,' *The Economic Times*, 14 Sep 2016, http://economictimes.indiatimes.com/news/defence/indiathreatened-by-china-myanmar-ties-chinese-thinktank/article show/54328467.cms

'IWAI inks pact with IPGPL for Kaladan multimodal transit work,' *Economic Times*, Jun 20, 2016 http://economictimes.indiatimes.com/articleshow/52837295.cms?utm_source=contentofinterest&utm_medium=text

Import Bank of India Working Paper, No. 23, 2013.

Joshua Kurlantzick, Obama Announces Aid Package To Myanmar Council for Foreign Relations, 24 November, 2012.

Jawaharlal Nehru Memorial Lecture delivered by Aung San Suu Kyi on 12 Nov 2012 at Vigyan Bhayan, New Delhi.

Kachin Refugees in China Forced to Return, *Mizzima News*, 24 Aug 2012.

'Myanmar's Ties with India, Japan, West Concern China,' *The Times of India*, 6 Jan 2013.

'Myanmar's Electoral Landscape', International Crisis Group, Asia Report, 28 April 2015.

'Myanmar Elections: What You Need to Know, AFP, 4 Nov 2015.

'Myanmar's 2015 General Elections Explained,' BBC News, 5 Nov 2015.

'Myanmar, A New Experience,' http://www.nationsonline.org/oneworld/myanmar.html.

'Myanmar's Friendship with China is no hindrance to its India Ties,' *South China Morning Post*, 30 Aug 2016, http://www.scmp.com/comment/insightopinion/article/2011104/myanmars-friendship-china-no-hindrance-its-india-ties

'Myanmar reject US criticism over ethnic conflict,' Agencies, Angola Press, Yangon, 26 Jan 2013.

'Myanmar Monks Back President's anti-Rohingya Plan, *The Jakarta Post*, Associated Press, 2 Sep 2012, Yangon.

'Making Sense of Myanmar,' *Livemint*, 13 Jun 2013.

Regional Environmental Forum. 2004. 'Advancing World Governance: Perspective From the Regional Environmental Forum for Mainland Southeast Asia.' REF II, Bangkok, Thailand.

Press Conferences of the Ministry of Foreign Affairs, Chinese Ministry of Foreign Affairs, November 29, 2011, December 2, 2011 and December 19, 2011.

People's Daily (2011), 'Western Media Enthusiastically Discusses the Myitsone dam Project—A Disgusting Smile from 'Observers,' 10 October, online: http://energy.people.com.cn/GB/15845413.html.

'Respect Myanmar Sovereignty, China Says After Trial.' Reuters. 12 August 2009. http://www.reuters.com/article/idUSTRE57B0O02 009081

'Realism in India-Myanmar Relations,' *Financial Express*, 15 September 2003, http://www.financialexpress. com/news/realism-in-indiamyanmar-relations/89520.

'Russia-China Oil Pipeline Opens,' 2 Jan 2011. bbc.co.uk http://www.bbc.co.uk/news/world-asia-pacific-12103865

Rand org, http://www.rand.org/blog/2015/08/aung-san-suu-kyis-trip-to-china-sino-myanmar-relations.html

'Shwe Gas and Pipeline Project-Myanmar,' Banktrack. http://www.shwe.org/archives/myanmar2013bangl adesh-india-gas-pipeline-bangladesh-is-preparingto-negotiate-without-conditions. Accessed on 29 April 2010.

'Thein Sein to Visit China,' *Mizzima News*, 4 Apr 2013.

'They Lose Elections'. *The Economist*, July 18, 2015, http://www.economist.com/news/asia/21657809-election-myanmar-may-produce-more-questions-answers-lose-lose-election

'US Sends Envoy to Myanmar,' Associated Press 26 Aug 2012.

UN Security Council, S/PV.5919, 12 January 2007.

United Nations. 2009. "UN Security Council Press Statement on Myanmar," SC 9731. 13 August.

Wikipedia, https://en.wikipedia.org/wiki/Myanmar.

Secondary Sources

Agnes Frittin and Niklas Swanström, 'European Sanctions Against Myanmar,' ISDP Policy Brief, No. 15, January 20, 2010.

Anand Kumar, 'Myanmar-Petrochina Agreement: A Setback to India's Quest for Energy Security,' South Asia Analysis Group, paper no. 1681, 19 January 2006, http://www.southasiaanalysis.org.

Andrew Selth (2001), 'Burma: A Strategic Perspective,' wp 13, The Asia Foundation.

Andrew Selth (2003), 'Burma's China connection and The Indian Ocean Region.' wp377, Australian National University.

Andrew Selth, 1995. "Asia, the Burmese Army.' *Jane's Intelligence Review*, 1 November: 84-125.

Asem Lalit, 'Road Equipment given to Myanmar,' *Imphal Free Press*, 22 May 2010.

Aung Hla Tun, 'Myanmar Govt., Rebels Sign Draft Nationwide Ceasefire Accord,' Reuters, 20 Mar 2015.

Aung Marm Oo, 'Indian Look East Policy and the Kaladan Project of Western Burma, www.mizzima.com, Jan 24, 2013.

Aye Thidar Kyaw, 'China Firms Trade positions in Myanmar,' *The Myanmar Times*, vol. 31, January 16–22, 2012; Aye Thidar Kyaw, 'Trade Volume to Jump 12 percent,' *The Myanmar Times*, March 28, 2011; Thomas Kean, 'Foreign Investments Flood into Myanmar,' *The Myanmar Times*, June 27, 2011.

Aye Win Myint, 'Myanmar Government Struggles to Contain Anti-Muslim Hostility,' *Meiktila*, 25 Mar 2013.

Ben Blanchard. 2010. 'Factbox: Pipeline From Myanmar to China to Carry Oil.' Reuters. 3 February. http://www.reuters.com/article/idUSTRE6120MQ2 0100203. Accessed on 2 May 2010.

Bertin Lintner (1998), 'Burma and its Neighbours. India's and Chinese

Foreign Policy in Comparative Perspective,'Radiant Publishers, New Delhi.

Bi Shihong, 'China-Myanmar Cooperation Won't be Hindered by India's Look East Policy,' *Global Times*, 23 Oct 2016, http://www.globaltimes.cn/content/1013168.shtml.

Bruce Gale, 'Military Still holds Wild Card in Myanmar,' *Straits Times*, 31 August 2012.

Cristina Garafola, "Sino-Myanmar Relations as the Countdown to the November Elections," The Rand Corporation, Aug. 2015.

D. M. Seekins, 'Burma-China Relations: Playing with Fire http://www.cnn.com/AIANOW/asiaweek/99/0528/nat4html; *International Herald Tribune*, 3 June 1997; *Asia 1996 Yearbook*, p. 97;,' op. cit., p. 534.

D. M. Seekins, 'Burma-China Relations: Playing with Fire,' ibid., p. 534.

Dai Yonghong and Wang Jianping, 'China and Myanmar: When Neighbours become Good Friends,' Sichuan University, 2015.

Dai Yonghong & Zhang Guoxuan, 'No Sign of a Sea Change for Myanmar's Foreign Policy,' *East Asia Forum* 23 Dec 2016, http://www.eastasiaforum.org/2016/12/23/no-sign-of-a-seachange-for-myanmars-foreign-policy/

Dai Yonghong and Wang Jianping, 'Suu Kyi Demonstrates Changing China-Myanmar Relations,' Sichuan University.

Daniel Ten Kate, 'Myanmar Seeks 'Win-Win-Win' in Balancing U.S.-China Competition,' Bloomberg, http://mobile.bloomberg.com/news/2011-12-04/myanmar seekswin-win-win-in-balancing-u-s-china-competition, December 4, 2012 (accessed March 14, 2012); Zhao Hong & Yang Mu, 'China-Myanmar Economic Corridor: Opportunities and Challenges,' EAI Background Brief, No. 670, October 27 2011, http://www.eai.nus.edu.sg/ BB670.pdf (accessed March 14, 2012).

Daniel Wagner, 'The Impact of Energy on China/Myanmar Relations,' *The Diplomat*, 2015.

David Arnott, 'China-Burma Relations, Challenges to Democratization in Burma.'

David Brewster, 'China's Pakistan project: a geopolitical game-changer,' *East Asia Forum*, 15 Dec 2016, http://www.eastasia

forum.org/2016/12/15/chinas-pakistan-project-a-geopolitical-game-changer/.

David I. Steinberg, 'China counter-pivots on Myanmar', *Asia Times.*

Dhruva Jaishankar, 'Myanmar is Pivoting away from China,' Foreign Policy Group, Washington DC. http://foreignpolicy.com/2015/06/15/myanmar-burma-is-pivoting-away-from-china-aung-san-suu-kyi-xi-jinping-india/

Dingding Chen, 'How Will Myanmar's Elections Affect Relations With China?' *The Diplomat*, 17 Nov 2015, http://thediplomat.com/2015/11/how-will-myanmars-elections-affect-relations-with-china.

Dipanjan Roy Chaudhury, 'India likely to boost ties with Myanmar; closely following outcome of Aung San Suu Kyi's China tour,' *The Economic Times*, 13 Jun 2015, http://economictimes.indiatimes.com/news/defence/india-likely-to-boost-ties-with-myanmar-closely-following-outcome-of-aung-san-suu-kyis-china-tour/articleshow/47650021.cms.

Dipanjan Roy Chaudhury, 'India to help modernise Myanmar Army and Navy to broad-base defence partnership,' *ET Bureau*,17 July 2015.

Dipanjan Roy Chaudhury, 'India to Help Modernise Myanmar Army and Navy to Broad-base Defence Partnership,' *The Economic Times*, 17 Jul 2015, http://economictimes.indiatimes.com/news/defence/india-to-help-modernise-myanmar-army-and-navy-to-broad-base-defence-partnership/articleshow/48111686.cms.

Doug Bandow, 'Military Rule In Burma,' CATO Institute, 2011.

Dr. Subhash Kapila, 'India's Look East Policy and South China Sea: Politico Strategic Dynamics-Analysis,' November 13, 2013.

Elizabeth Roche, 'Indian Analysts Welcome Democracy in Myanmar,' *Livemint*, Nov,10, 2015. http://www.livemint.com/Politics/pTmX1jE93B2oMBMq9AnImI/Indian-analysts-welcome-democracy-in-Myanmar.html.

Eric Draitser, 'Myanmar: Strategic Crossroads in Asia,' *Counter Punch*, 18 Nov 2015, http://www.counterpunch.org/2015/11/18/myanmar-strategic-crossroads-in-asia/

Eric Meyer, 'With Oil and Gas pipelines, China takes a Shortcut through Myanmar,' *Forbes Asia*, 2015.

Eunice Yoon, 'China Polishes Myanmar Relations as West Closes in,' CNBC, 15 Jun 2015.

Ge Hongliang, 'China-Myanmar Projects must be Equally Beneficial,' *Global Times*, 17 Aug 2016, http://www.globaltimes.cn/content/1000914.shtml.

Gwen Robinson & Geoff Dyer, 'White house Easing of Myanmar Imports Ban,' 13 Sep 2012.

Gwynne Dyer, 'Burma, The Generals Win Again,' *The Hitavad*, 10 July 2015.

Hiranya Saikia, 'India-Myanmar Relations— From Past to Present Scenario,' *Times of Assam*, 26 Aug 2014.

Hnin Yi, 'The Political Role of Military in Myanmar,' CAPS working Paper Series, RPD-13003, Ritumeikan Asia Pacific University, Jan 2014.

Hongwei Fan (2012). 'The 1967 anti-Chinese riots in Burma and Sino–Burmese relations,' *Journal of Southeast Asian Studies*, 43, pp 234-256. doi: 10.1017/S0022463412000045.

Ian Storey, 'Emerging Fault Lines in Sino–Burmese Relations: The Kokang Incident,' The Jamestown Foundation, China Brief, vol. 9, issue 18 (2009).

Indrani Bagchi, 'India, Myanmar agree to fight terrorism jointly,' *The Times of India*, 16 July 2015.

Jake Maxwell Watts, 'Myanmar: Airlines Fly in,' *Financial Express*, 11 Sep 2012.

John Cherian, 'Coming closer,' *Frontline* (Chennai), vol. 27, no. 17, 24-27 August 2010.

Jörn Dosch, 'China and Southeast Asia: A New Regional Order in the Making,' in *China, the Developing World, and the New Global Dynamic*. ed. Lowell Dittmer and George T. Yu (Boulder, Colo.: Lynne Rienner Publishers, 2010), 69.

K. Bradsher and J. Mouawad. 2005. 'China Oil Giants Crave Respectability and Power.' *New York Times*. 9 July. http://www.nytimes.com/2005/07/09/business/worldbusiness/09cnooc.html?pagewanted=1&_r=3 Accessed on 2 May 2010.

Kaladan Multimodal Transit Transport Project, 2015, www.gktoday.in.

Keling, Mohammad Nasir, Otto F Von, Mohd Na'eim & Md. Shukri, 'A Historical Approach to Myanmar's Democratic Process,' *Journal of Asia Pacific Studies* (2010), vol. 1, no. 2, 132-148.

Keling, Mohammad Nasir, Otto F Von, Mohd. Na'eim & Md. Shukri, 'A Historical Approach to Myanmar's Democratic Process,' *Journal of Asia Pacific Studies* (2010), vol. 1, no. 2, 132-148.

Kerstin Duell, 'Non Traditional Security Threats, International Concerns and Exiled Opposition, 2011. Internal Conflict in Myanmar,' Vij. Books, pp 47-49.

Kezia Dewi, 2009. 'Yunnan: Home of 25 Ethnic Minorities in China.' Associated Content. 30 March. http://www.associatedcontent.com/article/1593284/ yunnan_home_of_25_ethnic_minorities.html?cat=4 7. Accessed on 2 May 2010.

Khaing Kyaw Mya (2010), 'Indian border state envoys to tour Burma,' *Mizzima News* online, www.mizzima.com/business/4322-indian-border-state-trade-envoys-to-tour-burma.html.

'Kiran Sharma, 'Suu Kyi Rekindles Ties in India, Seeks Development Cooperation for Myanmar,' *Nikkei Asia Review*, 20 Oct 2016.

Larry Jagan, 2009, 'Border War Rattles China Myanmar Ties.' *Asia Times*. 1 September. http://www.atimes.com/atimes/Southeast_Asia/KI0 1Ae04.html

Li Chenyang, Presentation at the conference 'China and Myanmar: the Dilemmas of Mutual Dependence," Georgetown University, November 4, 2011.

Lien H Sakhong, 'The Future of Indo-Burma Relations.' View from Divided Peoples. 2010.

Manish Chand, 'India-Myanmar Ties: Buddha, Business and Bollywood,' MEA article, 10 Aug 2014.

Mary Callahan, 'The Endurance of Military Rule in Burma. Not Why, But Why Not?'

Mary P. Callahan, 'New Dragon or Still Dragging?' *Asian Survey*, vol. 35, no. 2, February 1995, p. 206.

Matthew Pennington, 'US Seeks Validation of Democratic Reforms as Myanmar Votes.' *Yahoo News*, 11 July 2015.

Matthew Pennington, 'US-Myanmar Military Ties Spark Unease,' *The Associated Press*, Sep 5, 2013.

Maung Aung Myoe, 'A Historical Overview of Political Transition in Myanmar Since 1988, Asia Research Institute, National University of Singapore, 2007.

Maung Aung Myoe. 2007. 'Sino-Myanmar Economic Relations Since 1988.' No. 86, Asia Research Institute, National University of Singapore, April.

Mitch Moxley, 'Rising Border Tension Threatens China–Burma Relations,' *The Irrawaddy*, May 20, 2012, http://www.irrawaddy.org/article.php?art_id=18508

Mohinder Pal Singh, 'Cementing Indo-Myanmar ties,' CLAWS web Article No. 2051 dated 20 Nov 2013.

Mohinder Pal Singh, 'Sino-Myanmar Relations and its Implications for India,' in *India's National Security in the 21st Century*, Eds. Prof Adhikari and Prof. Sanjeev Bhadauria, Pentagon Press, 2014.

Mohinder Pal Singh, 'The Myanmar – China Oil Pipeline: Implications for India,' CLAWS Web Articles No.1059, 2013.

Mohinder Pal Singh, 'Understanding Myanmar's Election, Skewed Constitution and its Conundrums,' *Economic and Political Weekly*, 7 Nov 2015.

Monique Skidmore & Trevor Wilson, 'Dictatorship, Disorder and Decline in Myanmar, Australian National University, Canberra, 2008.

Namrate Panwar, 2009, 'India and China Competing over Myanmar Energy,' University of Leicester, 14-16 December. pp.1-35 BISA Conference December 2009.

Nayanima Basu, 'India Inc's Next Big Destination: Myanmar,' 27 Jun 2013.

Nicolas Swanstrom, 'China-Myanmar Relations,' 2012.

Niharika Mandana, 'Indian Army Attacks Militant Camps in Myanmar,' *Wall Street Journal*, 10 Jun 2015.

Niklas Swanssrrom, 'Sino-Myanmar Relations: Security and Beyond,' Asia Paper, Institute for Security and Development Policy, 2012

Niklas Swanström & He Yin, 'China's War on Narcotics: Two Perspectives,' Caucasus–Asia Institute, Silk Road Studies Program, Silk Road Paper (December 2006).

Oken Jeet Sandham, 'Myanmar-based Militant Activities on Rise on Indian Side,' 26 April 2010, http:// www.e-pao.net/ GP.asp?src=11..260410.apr10.

Patrick Barta, 'Thousands Taken off Myanmar's Black List,' *Wall Street Journal*, 28 Aug 2012.

Peter James Spielman, 'UN to Myanmar: Make Rohingya Muslims Citizens,' United Nations, 19 Nov 2013. Associated Press.

Peter W. Rodman, 'China Woos Burma', *International Herald Tribune*, 30 May 1997, op. cit.

Poon Kim Shee (2002), 'The Political Economy of China-Myanmar Relations. Strategic and Economic Dimensions, *Ritsumeikan Annual Review of International Studies*. pp. 33-53.

Poon Kim SHEE, 'The Political Economy of China-Myanmar Relations: Strategic and Economic Dimensions,' 2002.

Priya Ravichandran, Indias Prospects with Myanmar, Live Mint, 14 Mar 2016, http://www.livemint.com/Opinion/fEorPG593mfp6uwiZHOu0L/Indias-prospects-with-Myanmar.html.

Rajat Pandit, 'India Steps up Military Aid to Myanmar to Offset China's Might,' *TNN*, Nov 1, 2013.

Rajat Pandit, 'Now Antony headed for Myanmar to Bolster Defence Ties,' *TNN*, Jan. 5, 2013.

Rakteem Katakey & James Paton, 'Myanmar as Economic Miracle Hinges on Natural Gas Bounty,' *Bloomberg Business*, 7 Jun 2013.

Shee Poon Kim, 'The South China Sea in China's Strategic Thinking,' *Contemporary Southeast Asia*, vol. 19, no. 4, March 1998, Singapore, pp. 369-387.

Shyam Saran, 'The Virtue of Pragmatism,' *The Times of India*, 7 August 2010.

Simon Roughneen, 'Burma's Economy can Triple by 2030: ADB,' *The Irrawaddy*, 21 Aug 2012.

Simon Roughneen, 'Burma's Emerging Democracy,' *The Irrawaddy*, 24 July 2012.

Soibal Dasgupta, 'Myanmar President U Thein Sein Calls Relationship with China Fraternal,' Times News Network, 25 Jul 2013.

Song Qingrun, 'China a Sincere Supporter of Myanmar's Pursuit of Peace and Reconciliation,' *Global Times*, 11 Dec 2016, http://www.globaltimes.cn/content/1023096.shtml.

Sridhar Ramaswamy & Tridivesh Singh Maini, 'The Strategic Importance of Myanmar for India,' August 12, 2014.

Stanley Weiss, 'What Myanmar Must do to Free Itself of China,' *Forbes Opinion*, 2 Sep 2013.

Stuart Chapman, 'Suu Kyi Concludes Four-Day Visit to India, Bilateral Relations Reinforced,' *Crowdh News*, 19 Oct, 2016.

Subir Bhaumik, 'Guns, Drugs and Rebels,' *Seminar* (New Delhi), no. 550, June 2005, http://www.indiaseminar.com/2005/550/550%20subir%20bhaumik.htm#top.

Sudha Ramachandra, 'China Secures Myanmar Energy Route," Asia Times Online, April 3, 2009, http://www.atimes.com/atimes/South_Asia/KD03Df03.html

Sudhir Bhowmik, 'Look East Policy: India Underperforming its Role in Myanmar,' 2 Oct 2013.

Sun, Yun (2012), 'China's Strategic Misjudgment on Myanmar,' *Journal of Current Southeast Asian Affairs*, 31, 1, 73-96.

T.B. Singh, 'A study on Indo-Myanmar Border Trade,' 2007.

Thomas Fuller and Wai Moe, 'Sectarian Clashes are Reported in Central Myanmar,' *New York Times*, 21 Mar 2013.

Thomas Kean, 'India looks to improve defence ties with Myanmar,' *Myanmar Times*, 17 July 2015.

Tridivesh Singh Maini, 'Myanmar and the India/China Shuffle,' *The Globalist*, 18 Oct 2015, http://www.theglobalist.com/myanmar-india-china-politics-south asia.

Tridivesh Singh Maini, 'Myanmar's Post-Election Future With India, 2016,' http://thediplomat.com/2015/11/myanmars-post-election-future-with-india/

'Thein Sein to Leave for US on Sept 24,' *Mizzima News* 12 Sep 2012.

Vicky Bowman, 'China Faces Tougher Laws in Myanmar,' *The Diplomat*, 17 Sep 2016, http://thediplomat.com/2016/09/china-faces-tougher-laws-in-myanmar.

Wilfried Arz, 'Geostrategic Importance of Burma/Myanmar Increasing,' 2011.

Wyatt Olson, 'US Marks Closer Ties with Myanmar, but China's Influence Lingers,' *Zuma Press*, Yangon.

Yadana Htun, 'Myanmar Government Ends Direct Media Censorship,' Associated Press, 20 Aug 2012.

Yun Sun, 'Gas Pains for China and Myanmar,' *Asia Times*, 2014.

Yun Sun, 'Myanmar in US China Relations,' *Stimson, Issue Brief*, No. 3, Jun 2014.

Yunnan Wang (2011), 'Six Strategic Priorities in the 12th Five Year Plan are related to Yunnan, 7 March, online: http://yn.yunnan.cn/html/2011-03/07/content_1521715. html.

Zhang Ye, 'Cross-border Railway Builds Ties,' *Global Times*, 17 Aug 2016, http://www.globaltimes.cn/content/1001090.shtml

INDEX